KARMIC
CONSEQUENCES

KARMIC
CONSEQUENCES

Discover your true self,
Establish a personal code of conduct

Arragokula Prudvi Raaj (Mangamma)

White Falcon Publishing

Karmic Consequences
Arragokula Prudvi Raaj

Published by White Falcon Publishing
Chandigarh, India

The contents of this book have been certified and timestamped
on the Gnosis blockchain as a permanent proof of existence.
Scan the QR code or visit the URL given on the back cover
to verify the blockchain certification for this book.

The views expressed in this work are solely those of the author
and do not reflect the views of the publisher, and the publisher
hereby disclaims any responsibility for them.

Requests for permission should be addressed to the publisher.

ISBN - 978-93-48199-61-4

PREFACE

Everything we do has consequences. We understand there are legal, social, political, and economic consequences. Even if we don't fully understand them, we can take the help of professionals for guidance. But when it comes to spiritual matters, often, there is a gap in essential information. There is truth, there is higher truth, there is higher truth… and there is ultimate truth liberation. You cannot lead one directly to ultimate reality without knowing where a person is. Often, those who preach in the name of spirituality exhibit moral superiority, which can lead to the development of weak individuals. Strong character doesn't evolve not because of the fear of pain or death; instead, it is the fear of righteousness, especially in early periods of life. It is the reason people turn into atheists at a young age, as they feel spirituality is too judgmental to the extent that they feel suffocated. We may not pay much attention to spiritual subjects, but they play a crucial role in our lives, directly or indirectly influencing many of our decisions, and those decisions shape every situation in our lives.

NAMAN

In my life, I went through a lot of psychological suffering at a young age due to a lack of clarity. Schools and colleges taught various sciences, but there was no study about life, death, and whether there is anything beyond. In my quest for truth, I often met people who tried to sway me to their beliefs. However, this nation is home to numerous insightful gurus who have illuminated my understanding of the world through their books, teachings, and training. I extend my heartfelt gratitude to all the gurus out there. Naman.

CONTENTS

CHAPTER 1

INTRODUCTION

In my childhood, once I wished to do something, my family members gave some consequences with a grave voice. In such a way that after listening to them, there was nothing left for me to think about anymore; I would do what they expected to be the best thing. However, I was planning to move further, and they didn't like it. I asked them what is the reason. Initially, they attempted reasoning but eventually resorted to a threat. Saying, "If you do it or engage in a certain action related to it, most likely you would suffer from ABC," and bringing more stuff from Puranas, "You know what happened in Mahabharata to a person who disrespected his brother." They tended to share lengthy stories. Those stories were beautiful and meaningful, but how they adapt is irrelevant. They do not get to see how an older brother could be sometimes. Later, on the other hand, it was a time in college when everyone at that age followed pop culture. Friends talk about cool stuff from science. Someone in class is a favorite student of the science teacher, and they go on talking about how most of the things from religion are stupid nonsense. If you follow something from tradition that is not so common in the surroundings, you are a fun thing to watch.

Sometimes, I have been a stubborn idiot in my elders' eyes, and sometimes, I've been a stupid orthodox friend in my circle. By disregarding elders and traditions, they deemed me foolishly stubborn, and in some cases, they were right. By following what I have learned from my family and culture, the people my age could not relate to it. They look at me as an awkward orthodox. Perhaps they, too, were right at times. I suffered a lot in trying to figure out the exact line between science and tradition or spirituality. I often question whether a line exists, as one subject contradicts another.

How do we distinguish between what is good and what is bad? For a long time, I have found it difficult to comprehend what is right and wrong, correct or incorrect, and appropriate or inappropriate. No matter what I do, someone always comes up with a more extensive and logical explanation of how I am wrong. Even those who preach to me are imperfect in the eyes of their elders.

After a lot of calculations, I arrived at a conclusion. Consider where you are now and where you wish to reach. Evaluate how you are doing now and what you want to become. Based on that, what is helping you reach the desired point and transform into the person you want to be is good for you. That which is not helping, but instead taking you away from the point you wish to reach, is bad for you. There is nothing like a good thing or a bad thing. Essentially, there are only helpful things and not-so-useful things. I do not mean to dismiss all the virtues of life. It bases everything that is good or bad on our desires, goals, and achievements we set for ourselves. Then how can we have so many rules and moral scriptures, such as the Sacred Sin? Instead, they are just consequences.

Imagine you are going somewhere and making a big decision in your life; you see some pleasure and happiness in it. Whatever it is that you are trying to derive joy from is leading to some consequences. If you are willing to face the consequences, you will go further; otherwise, you will not. The question is, how have you arrived at all the potential outcomes? They are based on your current perception and understanding of the world and situations. This is where Hinduism/Sanathana and many religions come into existence. They provide another level of consequences to which most people are unaware.

We consider there are four types of consequences:

1) Legal consequence: Do your actions break someone's rights or some legal obligations? 2) Social consequences: What you do may be within the law, but society may still treat you in a certain way. 3) Political consequences: It's everywhere; you are planning something, your parents are planning something, and your brother is planning something else, though all are planning for family well-being. 4) Economic consequences: Profit loss, debt, and

credit. We also think there are some moral values. Are they really moral values? No, they are not precisely morals, only consequences, but of another level: 5) spiritual or karma consequences. But how accurate are the karma consequences, and what is the reasoning behind them? We will see in later chapters.

***

A young man in his early twenties desires something in his life. To achieve his desires, he makes a plan to the best of his knowledge, knowledge that he gained through his life experience. Achieving what he desires involves some action, which leads to certain consequences. He foresees four consequences: A, B, C, and D. After analyzing all potential outcomes, he makes his plans and proceeds further. An older man has gone through similar experiences to what the young man is planning to do. He foresees additional consequences, E and F, and many times, this young man would not have pursued what he desired, or at least he would have approached it differently at a different time with more preparation if he had been aware of the consequences of E and F. So when people say to listen to others, especially elders, it doesn't mean to obey their choices; instead, it means to know more about potential outcomes. However, this is only one side of the coin. There is another side to this.

A schoolboy is taking his 10th exams; something is true for him. A young man who has just graduated from college has a different perspective on the truth of life. There is a middle-aged man who has 10 years of work experience, is married with kids, and has his own version of the truth of life. Lastly, an elderly man in his 70s perceives life differently from the younger generations. Every time, the elder explains the truth about life to the younger. Often, the younger is incapable of understanding what the elder is saying because they do not see life through the other person's life experience and memory. Even if they come to understand intellectually, they cannot come to terms with their elders. Often, the younger goes through a lot of suffering; the schoolboy is so ashamed of not being able to understand what the young man is trying to teach him.

It is like there is one famous quotation in one sentence; it contains significant meaning. A schoolboy reads it; he makes some meaning out of it. Not that he doesn't understand. If the same person reads the quotation after 20 years, he will appreciate the depth of the sentence. People cannot know until they go through some experience and relate that experience to what has been said. Everyone is in a different state of evolution. Similarly, people are at varying levels of Karmik evolution, and based on that, they seek different things in various lives.

The general theory of relativity, by Albert Einstein, is scientifically proven, and this theory overrides Isaac Newton's law of gravity. However, even in space programs, we use Newton's laws of gravity. The theory of relativity comes into use only when traveling near the speed of light. Newton's law of gravity is 99.99% correct. Despite being incorrect, we use the law of gravity in our daily routines in many forms. Similarly, everyone is in a different state of being, and each individual has a different reality and truth. You hold that as truth for some time and move further when you finish it.

Success means a unique combination of various things to each individual. There is no generalized thing for success, but we are trying to generalize what success means, like working on a high-paying job, running a business, owning a luxurious car, building, etc. So we are supposed to work hard and achieve all those things, and then we get recognition as successful people. The higher you place yourself, the more people will consider you successful. In this nation (India), whatever the work you do and things and situations you like, the end goal has always been liberation. People seek different things in their lives; each sees life's fulfillment as unique. However, those who were enlightened and who knew life beyond death saw everything as a stepping stone towards a higher possibility, liberation. People may say they don't seek any liberation or spiritual experience, but one day they will. It may happen by the end of life or after many lifetimes. The enlightened masters and gurus have observed patterns in which people seek things and life experiences. No particular method or way of living applies to all, so they have made a few categories of systems based on the sequencing. So they don't deviate from themselves, so they don't keep rotating at the same point.

CHAPTER 1.1. WHY SHOULD YOU CONSIDER KARMIC CONSEQUENCES?

1. Fear of righteousness and its role in forming character.

Have you ever heard of people using dark magic or occult practices to control another person? There are stories of individuals using such practices on their family members out of love to seek their well-being. Because the person was so rebellious, they were going out of control to the extent that their survival was in question. Let's assume such a thing is possible. What happens when a person controls someone through such actions? The victim loses their defense mechanisms to a significant extent. By defense mechanisms, I mean that which preserves what you identify as yourself and for which you are willing to fight and die to maintain. Now, if not their family members, anyone can control them and lead them in any direction because their defense mechanism is broken. The person doing this for their well-being should take care of them forever. Every person has some defense mechanism, whether highly educated or illiterate. People undergo some education and some life experiences. Whatever they internalize, information is solidified, and they identify those things as themselves. Similarly, elders, lecturers, and well-wishers also dismantle the defense mechanism, if not by occult practices, then through their knowledge, intelligence, and sense of righteousness. They often say they are concerned about the younger students they are teaching, but there is pride in saying, "I am more right than you."

It's like the person is a circle that is sucking in information from their surrounding environment. It could be in the form of observing people and taking a few traits from them, reading books, watching movies and television, and so on. Later, this circle identifies the things that have gone into it, such as itself, and responds to its surroundings based on these things.

When I was 12 years old, I used to speak and act without much thought. I was confident, lively, and had a rhythm in my behavior that amused those around me. However, this changed later on. I became more passive and reserved because my defense mechanism was broken. It was necessary because if I had just made myself or solidified myself with whatever limited information I had at that time, I would have been a fool. I needed to gain more knowledge about the outside world to rebuild myself. A few years later, I tried to make myself again since I had gained some sense of knowing the outside world; again, I was proven wrong and felt humiliated. Any attempts to do something and feel some sense of autonomy were far away; I felt like I couldn't do anything without following someone else's opinion. Sometimes, we take some people as our role models and try to imitate them. For example, students take their favorite teacher as a role model. We take some information from them and feel superior because most of what we say comes from the teacher. Everything is right, and everyone should obey. The teacher is knowledgeable but is still limited. There, you are also proven wrong, if not by the students, then by another teacher. When it's confusing and doesn't allow us to make ourselves, it is not about outside situations but inside will; what should be the action? It feels like no soul is inside; it is just a day of wandering, a passive person. Passiveness is the trait of remaining inactive and lacking initiative.

How we lack initiative.

Sometimes, my friends would take me out and say, "This is the best movie we are going to watch, this is the place we are going, this is the best food," etc. They are often correct, but sometimes, they are entirely wrong. Even when I knew they were wrong, I didn't dare to say so because they talked so confidently about what they believed, so I thought they must know something I did not know. Why this fear of being wrong? Because it was a time when the circle had no definitive boundaries. It's a time with significant information but no boundaries and no direction. You cannot even believe the information you have; who knows, someone could prove you a fool again. You might have often felt that what you thought was best later seems stupid. Because who you are is changing, or else we say you have not taken a rigid form. The outside world could have many possibilities, but inside you is fixed; if it has taken a standard form, you would be comfortable and peaceful. But that is never the intention of any guru; they want to dilute and dissolve you.

No one is weak, and no one is a loser; the only thing is that they are just confused. There is no such thing as not being able to fight for something until your death. You do not want to hear anyone saying, "If I were in your position, I would have done nothing like this because of so-and-so reason. How stupid you are to get into such things, etc." You fear others' views more, and they may defer your choice or provide more logical reasoning for what you should do in that specific situation. You are struggling between life's desires and not wanting to be a fool in your society, and you do not wish to do anything inappropriate. But the thing is, they do not know where you are and what you see as fulfillment in your life. To tell you what will help you.

Fear of righteousness could be reasonable and even necessary, but a clear vision of the self and the world should accompany it. Strong character doesn't evolve only because of the fear of pain or death; instead, it is the fear of righteousness, especially in the early periods of life. There is truth, and there is higher truth, and there is higher truth... and there is ultimate truth liberation. You cannot lead directly to the ultimate reality. You have to go step by step. People must live on a step for some time so they can evolve and gain the capability to climb higher steps. What is happening is random; people are teaching from different steps to anyone without knowing where this person is standing and expecting them to climb on the same step. This person is ashamed of being unable to live up to their standards.

2. Confidence is being at ease with oneself.

Learning body language and communication skills, along with slightly modulating the voice to appear confident, don't work because they do not come from within. People engage in many activities and take courses to boost their confidence because it is closely related to an individual's success. Using these tricks may initially portray an image of high confidence, but eventually, people come to know the truth. The real essence lies deep within who you are: your core values and belief system. Essentially, it is about who you hold yourself to be and how you see, perceive, and respond to the world.

People with a graduation and post-graduation degree working in a pleasant company with a high-paying job also suffer from an inferiority complex. Sometimes, it comes from not knowing something; the problem is they are unaware of what they don't know and should know. To fill this knowledge void, they read books, such as psychology and philosophy self-help books. Every piece of information fills the vacuum in their head, and one fine day, they get to know something that helps them see the big picture. They learn how things work in life, and their absolute confidence emerges. What I say, for many, is that the thing that makes the complete circle is spirituality. People have a good idea about how life works in the outside world. They get stuck in unrealistic moral values that they do not believe in from their heart. And some lame spiritual consequences, like if you commit this sin, God will give you punishment. Most people do not have any faith in heaven and hell. Still, they see something spiritual beyond this life and death—it is like missing information. When people are in confusion, there is no truth in them, and they suffer from an inferiority complex.

If you are a wall and there are missing bricks, causing air pockets, the wall cannot stand. It may stand, but it cannot withstand the environmental forces. It is like playing cards; every player calculates in their own way and at their own speed. People bid their money after some time. Player A bids after five moves, and at that time, whatever information is available to him seems good enough to bid. Player B needs more information before making a move. He feels like he is in darkness. There isn't enough light to make a move. According to Player B's calculations, there are many potential outcomes. They may be remote, but they exist.

You are shaped by your desires, and confidence comes from being comfortable with who you are.

Sometimes, twisted views on spirituality criticize your desires, leading to self-judgment and discomfort. Many young people become atheists because they feel judged by spirituality. You may not pay much attention to the spiritual subject, but it plays a prominent role in daily life. Directly or indirectly, it influences many of your decisions, which shape every situation in your life.

3. Decision making and suffering

Life is all about making decisions; you could be in any situation. Imagine there is a new colleague in your office. You do not have any information about him. You took his pen without his permission and lost it somewhere, and now you are anxious; there is some fear of how he might react. But still, you have an idea. What is possible? In a worst-case scenario, what could happen for a pen taken without permission? But what if the pen you lost is a gift from his mother, who passed away in his childhood? Many emotions and feelings are attached to it, making a huge difference. You do not know whether he is going to scold you, use abusive words, or slap you. You have no idea what could happen or what the potential outcomes are. This uncertainty is what's causing your anxiety.

In another situation, you are doing something for which your colleague is going to kill you for sure. But still, if there is a need to fulfill it even at the cost of your life, you would do it. And there won't be any hesitation or fear. So, you are suffering not from the outcome but mainly from the decision-making process. What you are paying is worth what you are going to receive. It's like wagering.

A problematic situation arises in your life, and you must make a big decision. You see it coming after a week and are thinking about the best thing to do; that day arrives. You are not sure, but you make a choice. It's been ten days, but even ten days later, you still question whether it was the right choice. You may have gone through a similar situation. From one week before to ten days after, you are suffering. What option would lead to the best outcomes? Even after deciding. Sometimes, it's not the outcome that causes the stress but rather the decision-making process. You do something that you later regret and think of yourself as foolish because your intelligence will hurt you if you do something silly. When you don't have clarity over the spiritual self, you do not know what you want, and the consequences could be a hell of suffering.

"You should have a hierarchy of values; otherwise, you will be painfully confused." - Jordan Peterson.

"Fool is somebody who doesn't have the right kind of priorities in his life." - Robert Greene.

Hierarchy means one thing is more important than others; otherwise, too many options can be confusing.

Each individual has a different hierarchy of values and needs. Most education is about providing many outcomes; however, very little education focuses on narrowing the options and choosing one that suits a person's unique needs.

4. Missing spiritual mentorship.

There are children who are very young, nine years and twelve years old, and they are doing well in arts, sports, and science, solving high-level mathematical theorems, which seems impossible to an average person, but I believe it is highly possible. However, when I see even a teenager, not a child, who talks like a wise old man, it's tough to believe because wisdom comes with age. If not age, at least through life experiences. Some people neither have age nor life exposure to various things. They live in a bubble of their universe but still talk wisdom. I wonder how it is even possible. Later, I found that it is often through mentoring, and sometimes it is high karmic evolution.

There is a giant skull, and within the skull, there are three small skulls, and in each small skull, there are three smaller skulls. Mentorship goes on from giant skulls to small skulls and from small skulls to smaller skulls. So they know what they want and what needs to be done in any situation. But now, every skull is evolving by itself without any guidance. Because people live in small families and have limited interactions with the community, it takes a long time to get an overview and understand the world comprehensively.

"What you are suffering is not your bondage; what you are suffering is your freedom." - Sadhguru.

Previously, there was no education; people did what their parents and grandparents did. There was no confusion because there were no options to think about. Many suffered during those times because they could not pursue their desires, but many were fine. We are blessed to live in a democracy where education is accessible to everyone; there is this freedom that anyone can be anything. Many enjoy this freedom, but some suffer from the same liberty because some instinctively know what they want while others don't. Some take time to figure out what they want, and some of their minds are, in a way, expecting someone to tell them what they should do if not imposed.

Some skulls have an idea if their elders from the family or community are not their larger skull, but they can choose the skull they want to be, and they can select their mentor based on their dreams.

Whenever someone tells you they want to say something good to you, you often think they will say something that leads to your desired point. However, usually, the person has existing characteristics, opinions, and views; based on that, they can only judge your desired point. Rarely do we encounter someone who is not judgmental, warns you about outcomes, and is still willing to help you. In this culture, there are many stories where demons went and asked their guru something that was terrible for them and others. Initially, the guru explained that their wish could be better. But later, the guru told the demon, "OK, it is your karma to suffer all these." They gave them a milder version of what they were seeking or something that reduced the impact. In a way, they were satisfying themselves at the same time, creating an ecological balance.

5. Relationships - Female and Male Nature

Females lean towards water, while males lean towards earth. Earth represents the assertion of firmness and rigidity. Women are adaptable, like water, and can take any form, while they prefer their men to be in a stable form. Imagine two bubbles — one representing a man and the other a woman — merging into one. After merging into one, the remains represent the man, while the representation of the woman dissolves. It does not mean that the woman ceases to exist, but rather that she plays a significant role inside the visible boundaries. Man is boundaries, not restricting but protecting. Women are creations, and the boundaries set by men are for the protection of women and their creations. Women have the freedom to choose whose boundaries they feel protected by, not restricted. However, if men and women do not know their priorities, then they suffer. Often, distorted spirituality does not allow the man to stand on his terms and women to choose the one. It's not only about men; even women suffer with men who don't know where he is heading and who don't have a clear view of his priorities and boundaries.

Long philosophy

As per a study by Dunning and Kugur, people are not good at evaluating themselves. The least skilled individuals are most likely to overrate themselves. People with moderate expertise will have less confidence in their beliefs, as they know enough to realize that there is a lot they don't know.

Four things are taught to a person; he internalizes the information and incorporates them into his life. Eight things are taught to another person, and he understands them and makes them part of his life. To another person, 24 different things are taught; doing the 1st thing at a particular time violates the 7th. Doing the 5th in a specific context violates the 13th one. This can make it difficult for them to solidify their character and can make them feel insecure and unsure about themselves.

The one who knows very little and stops their search at that point tends to have greater confidence, while those who have gone deeper and learned many things may lose their confidence, thinking they know nothing. This is where we Indians are: Arjuna, a fickle mind. Because of long philosophies and different cultures, many traditions and cultures contradict each other.

6. Uncertainty means fear and anxiety; a confused person can never have certainty.

We all desire money and spend it on insurance such as life, health, and property. We dedicate our time and energy to education and skill development due to uncertainty. This uncertainty brings fear and anxiety, so we work hard to earn money and learn new skills. We use our abilities and resources to create a more stable life. When we have certainty, we feel at peace. However, without certainty, fear and anxiety take over. It's hard to feel certain without understanding your spiritual self. In other words, no situation feels specific to you if you lack a solid foundation for certainty.

According to science, confusion is uncertainty about what is happening, intended, or required. Confusion can also be described as disorientation, which is losing one's sense of direction and having difficulty focusing. It also affects judgmental behavior, causing trouble making decisions. Clinical confusion might lead to difficulty carrying out tasks, a poor attention span, unclear speech, and difficulty following a conversation.

CHAPTER 2

COLLECTIVE SELF

There is a puzzle image on the dias, and the hall is full of audience members, but there are missing pieces. The audience has a task to figure out the picture, step by step, revealing the missing pieces. One person sitting in the right corner of the hall asks to reveal the A and C missing pieces because he feels those are the pieces that he needs to understand the picture. Another person sitting in the left corner of the hall sees it from a different angle. He wishes to uncover pieces F and G to figure out the picture.

Similarly, we all go through specific life experiences from which we try to figure out life and make some meaning. Different people requested to uncover unique pieces to figure out the picture, which doesn't make the revealed pieces in the picture any less important. However, people place more importance on those pieces that they learned after many struggles. The lessons learned after a series of struggles that we remember for the long term may be lifelong, and many of those lessons are beautifully turned into quotes. Especially if they come from a highly successful person, we pay more attention to them, but we can't say we can adapt them to our lives. This could be why you feel spirited when reading a quote for some time, and it often fades away. It would be best to understand the core subject; I am not slandering the quotes. They are quite good and could provide deep insight into the subject. Spirituality is a vast subject; listing a few things as spiritual consequences may seem the same as me writing quotes, so first, we will go through the core subject. Then you can identify the missing pieces; however, I have a long list of karmic consequences that concern me.

In India, spiritual exploration starts with questions and introspection. You may be familiar with the famous question from Ramana Maharshi, "Who am I?" People often identify themselves with different things, which can be categorized into two: 1. Collective self 2. Individual self.

There is a man who is 6 feet tall and weighs 70 kg. He looks at himself and feels a desire to grow and become more. One day, he gets married and feels complete with his wife by his side. They have children, and he thinks that his family is his identity. Later, he earns money and buys a house and property, which he believes are a part of him. He then starts a business and builds a large organization with thousands of employees. He feels that this organization and everything it encompasses is his identity. Then, he fights a battle and becomes the king of an extensive empire. He thinks this is me, including his wife, children, kingdom, and property. Even after being a king, taking the biggest and most significant man's identity, he still feels unfulfilled. Finally, he climbs a mountain, practices yoga meditation, and does some Sadhana to erase the boundaries of his individuality. By doing so, he experiences Brahman, in which there is no difference between him and everything else in the universe. This is what we refer to as Brahman or Vishwaroopam. When Lord Krishna showed Vishwaroopam to Arjuna in the Mahabharat, it wasn't that Lord Krishna became more extensive; instead, he gave Arjuna an experience of the universe within himself.

Let me rephrase the text to make it easier to understand with the help of a diagram.

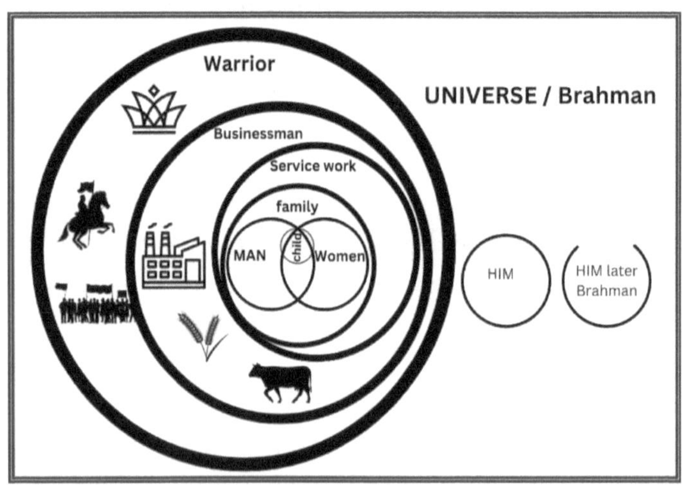

Illustration 1.

In the illustration, the circle representing a man meets with a circle representing a woman leading to the creation of a family. The family engages in a basic service-oriented occupation, thus establishing the shudra circle (Varna/caste is not determined by birth, instead it is determined by the nature of the individual. we will explore this varna concept in upcoming chapters). Later, the man started trade and agriculture, expanding his circle; now this circle includes several employees, animals, farms, and property, which forms a bigger circle, representing the Vysya. The man later engages in battles, emerges victorious in a war, and eventually ascends to the throne as the ruler of an empire. Now, including all family property businesses and a big kingdom that accommodates many people, he forms the enormous ellipse Kshatriya. Even if he is the empire's king, it is so tiny compared to the universe. What was a small circle now became this big Kshatriya by increasing his identity or territory line. First, he went on an increasing boundary line. He wanted to include more in it and have some control over them, but still, it couldn't settle him. Then, he climbs a mountain and does some Yoga, pooja, and kriya. Through these methods, he erased the boundaries of all kinds of identification.

On the right side of the diagram, there is a small circle labeled "him." This circle represents the individual continually expanding his circle size by incorporating many things into himself. Next to this circle is a half-made circle or a circle with erased boundaries, representing Brahman. As long as the line meets its starting point and makes a complete circle, you can differentiate between what is inside the boundary as "him" and what is outside as other. However, once a person erases the borders, there is no discrimination between the individual and others. They see everything as one entity. Brahmacharya refers to the actions one performs to reach the ultimate. Being celibate could be one part of Brahmacharya to conserve energy, but it is not everything. Only those who attain Brahman can end their quest to include more and more things in themselves.

Let us go through these concepts in depth.

My hands are a part of me; I need my hands. I can do various things with them as I have trained my hands in multiple skills over years of practice. Now, there is a significant dependency on my hands, and if I were to lose my hands, it would cause me pain and suffering. If I had not had my two hands since childhood, I would have developed a distinct set of skills and unique behavior patterns that would enable me to survive without them. Since I have lived with my hands and with the hope that my hands would remain intact with my body until death, there is now a significant dependency on my hands, and because of this dependency, I suffer. Who I am, the boundary line is my entire body, not my hands and remaining body separate.

Similarly, in a relationship, two people function as one entity and depend on each other for various physical, emotional, psychological, and economic needs. Losing a partner can cause immense suffering, similar to losing a limb. In some cases, one person may be the life force of the relationship, like the heart, and the other person cannot survive without them. This raises the question of whether parents are a person's heart. While parents are not a person's heart, a child is the heart of their parents. Parents may act as the spine of the child, and genetics is not the only reason why a child is the heart of their parents. There are various levels and layers to this dynamic.

In some movies, there is a typical scene where the hero fights off a group of villains. As the hero is about to kill the main villain, the villain's wife suddenly appears and begs for mercy. The hero then spares the villain's life. This scene may be ingrained in our minds due to various traditions that teach us that by killing someone, we are not only taking their life but also taking away a part of their loved ones. Therefore, the hero's mercy is not for the villain but for his wife.

Your hand is a part of you; you will let it be a part of you as long as you have some control over it. If your hand doesn't listen to your instructions and starts hurting you, first you try all the ways to control it. But if it doesn't listen to you and starts poking your eyes and squeezing your neck, then you have to separate your hand from your body, no matter how dear your hand is to you. This is why people often fight with those they love the most; it's a struggle between dependency and control. You say you love someone because there is dependency, and you fight the same for control. In a relationship, control is necessary to know if the other person is a part of your life. If you don't have any control over your hand, you don't know if it's a part of you. You doubt whether they exist within your circle's boundary line.

If you cut your fingers, it is painful for you because it is in your sensations. Your fingers are part of you. If your child cuts his fingers, it also pains you, but not exactly in the same way it does to your fingers. If you lose some property at a distance, it pains you in another way. So what you are most concerned about is your identity. As discussed in the previous diagram, you are happy when the circle you consider yourself to be in is increasing. When it is decreasing, you are unhappy. You feel the happiest when everything within the circle is going well but become sad when it is not. Sometimes, what is outside the circle is beneficial, and you are not; then, you are unhappy out of envy. As long as the circle that you consider yourself to be in is moving in the direction where you are heading, you are happy. You are unhappy if anyone inside the circle moves in the opposite direction. As long as there is discrimination between what you are and what is the other, there is happiness and unhappiness; once you erase this discriminatory part, there won't be any happiness, sadness, or sorrow.

The head of a family is responsible for all family members, and controlling the family can be complicated since everyone is evolving. It would help to consider your entire family before making any decisions that could affect them. People could be wholly independent and devoid of family relationships; however, this is impossible for most people. In childhood and early teens, they were okay with some relationships, but as they grew up and their needs increased, they chose partners who fulfilled those needs based on their individual requirements.

If a family is a collective body, you could be the head; likely, you could be the head of some part of society. The head of the collective body is changing over time. You just got the chance to be the head for some time. Kingdoms, people, and properties are not you; all could be yours, but how long? Someone will come and take your place. Many seek to expand their horizons to fill the void left by these possessions, but one day, they choose to eliminate these boundaries. But how does one erase the circle, and where are the boundaries to erase? Each person may need to address five different layers of identity.

CHAPTER 3

INDIVIDUAL SELF

Before we explore individual identities, we will need to examine the concept of karma.

KARMA

A soft drink machine dispenses flavored drinks when a coin is inserted. The machine offers ten different flavors but randomly selects one without giving the user a choice. Let's imagine a man who has never tried a flavored drink before and uses the machine three times within a certain period. By coincidence, he receives only the least-liked flavor, type X, each time he uses the machine. The fourth time he uses the machine, he only wants the type X flavor. If he gets a different flavor, he will most likely be disappointed. Even though type X is not the best flavor, and he has not tasted any other flavor, he has developed a preference for it due to his previous experiences. In this culture, we say that if someone is suffering, it is their karma.

When we say karma, no one admits to having done something wrong, so someone is punishing them, or that outside nature is doing something to them. They have tasted one type of flavor. It's gone so deep into them that they cannot accept anything other than that—the nonacceptance is what they are suffering from. Karma means action; everything you do is karma, and everything you do not do by will is also karma. Everything you do repeatedly goes deeper into the mind, and this memory will decide the remaining life. Anything similar to the existing memory will be allowed, and anything unfamiliar will be met with resistance. It may not revolt, but it isn't easy to accept new things. Their inability to accept new things into their lives due to the existing memory is what they are suffering from. Karma is just repetitive memory on various levels. Karma is good when you need a skill to deal with repetitive work. However, it becomes a burden when we need to learn new skills, as we must overwrite existing ones. So, we must be aware of our actions, as they shape our lives and determine how we respond to new situations.

Another example: An unemployed person living in a cheap apartment, searching for a job, accidentally gets to stay in a star hotel. It's a luxurious hotel with many facilities. However, he could not sleep at night because, in the place where he lives, there were all kinds of noises, such as a husband and wife shouting, a person watching a movie loudly, and some carpenters working. As a result, he could not sleep in the star hotel, which was completely silent. Then he goes back to his apartment with a tape recorder. He records all the noises and plays the same tape in his new hotel. Only then could he sleep.

As collective identities fade, individual identity remains. Individual identity is said to exist in five different layers.

1. Annamaya kosha.

    Annamaya Kosha is the outer layer of the body—the physical body, or what you call the food body. The body comes from food, and food comes from soil.

    At first, people identify themselves by name, origin, profession, and other factors. However, eventually, they begin to identify themselves by their physical body. This body, which people consider themselves, is a product of their genetic memory. Food transforms into a human body in a unique way based on genes. Even within the same species, every creature is unique. Each individual also has a unique personality. It's not just the memory of the food that creates this uniqueness, but also the arrangement of the food. Since many creatures consume the same food, each has a distinct biochemical arrangement. This is the reason that every individual is unique.

    Yogis use the concept of the five elemental transactions to describe their connection with the universe. We are not separate from the rest of the universe but a part of it. We have five senses, through which we are in continuous contact with the universe.

Yes, we can see because we have eyes, but more so because of sunlight or fire. Our ability to see depends on the presence of light, which carries information that our eyes detect and process.

We have a sense of taste because we have a tongue, and our sense of taste depends on water. Once we chew food, saliva mixes with the food and brings the chemical information of the food to the tongue. The transmission of food information occurs through the water. Without water, we cannot perceive the sense of taste.

Similarly, because there is air, we have a sense of smell. And our body is just a creation of soil. These are some examples of how the body is in continuous transaction with the universe.

2. Manomaya kosha Mind Memory

Our personality is the Manomay kosha, which encompasses our feelings, desires, ideas, and overall happiness or unhappiness. It is often compared to a monkey, as it engages in unnecessary and endless actions. Reading and surrounding ourselves with good company can enhance our memory, which benefits the Manomay. However, negative emotions such as Rage (Krodha), Greed (Lobha), Pride (Madha), and Lust (Kama) can hurt the Manomay.

People often introduce themselves by sharing their occupations and accomplishments, which are part of their psychological memory. If someone says, "I am my mind," this also refers to memory in a different sense. The mind is a collection of thoughts that accumulates over time.

Emotions and Feelings

Emotions are for immediate survival needs; they alert us to immediate dangers. Like when we see a lion, we get scared. This fear triggers an automatic reaction that helps us stay safe. According to science experts, emotions carried by the limbic brain evolved to act upon a specific stimulus. A neural impulse moves an organism to action, prompting automatic reaction behavior that has been updated through evolution as a survival mechanism. Feelings, on the other hand, play a role in long-term survival. Feelings alert us to expect dangers and prepare for action. Feelings are the mental associations and reactions to an emotion that are personal and gained through experiences. Feelings vary from person to person and situation to situation because they are shaped by individual temperament and experiences. They tell us how to live by shaping our responses to future events.

Animals live on their instincts. Ever wonder why dogs chase running cars like mad? They perceive fast-moving objects as potential threats when moving in their territory; that is why they attack bicycle riders and joggers. This instinct has been passed down to dogs from their ancestors, possibly dating back hundreds of thousands of years. Now, we try to explain to the dog that we live in a civilized society and that there is no need to do such a thing anymore. Will the dog ever understand what you are saying? Humans have consciousness, which means they can choose what should be on the list of survival and what we should ignore. The way we learned to use fire and other dangerous elements is an example of consciousness; our instincts tell us to run away from them.

There is a wild species of snake found in the African jungle. Once it is born, it does not stay with its mother; within 2 hours, it goes on hunts, eats, and eventually reproduces one day. It does not take any lessons from its mother, nor does it practice. Scientists suggest it is one of the most evolved creatures in the wild because it instinctively knows what is necessary to survive at birth. You can domesticate a lion, but you cannot domesticate a python because they live in an intense survival loop. Humans live in a society where the outside world and societal norms constantly change. Any particular survival method cannot be installed for long-term survival (over generations); it cannot be passed down genetically. The skills needed for survival were different 1,000 years ago, different 25 years ago, and now require a completely different set of skills. Humans have some privileged space where certain things are standard, but there is scope for change. What is necessary for survival in this life? We learn in the early periods of our lives. A part of survival mechanisms is in the form of thoughts, strategies, and tactics. Some thoughts go so deep that they convert into feelings. When your feelings get hurt, it triggers the emotion, and in emotion, you have a different chemistry that enables you to come out of that problem. You make those decisions you would never make in your normal state of mind. Since feelings form through individual life experiences, strengths, weaknesses, and thinking, they vary from person to person.

Feelings, emotions, and thoughts are interrelated, or we say interdependent. When a feeling is hurt, it triggers an emotion, whereas that feeling itself is created by emotion. For example, a child who has a bad experience with a corrupt policeman may develop negative feelings towards the police. Another child who was saved by the police will likely develop positive feelings towards them. Experiencing fear in certain circumstances may lead to feelings that prompt avoidance of similar situations in the future. A child can avoid the problem, alert the defense mechanism, and implement a strategy to deal with that circumstance. Thoughts and repetitive thoughts can turn into feelings, and when a feeling is hurt, it triggers an emotion, which activates a different type of chemistry for survival. Emotional disharmony occurs when existing thoughts are turned into feelings that conflict with new thoughts representing current survival needs.

Why do you feel empathy towards the children? And why are you willing to die for them?

We cannot live in this world forever; even a 75-year lifespan is not a guarantee. We live in this world through children, so they are like an extension of our lives. When you see a child in trouble, you feel compelled to do everything you can to help them, sometimes even risking your life. Without empathy towards children, the chances of survival decrease, even if the child is not our own. Thoughts can be fickle and ever-changing. If we live with no emotions and feelings, relying solely on pure thoughts, and a person does not have control over his thoughts, what would be the survival rate? So nature doesn't trust you with your thoughts. For example, if a person commits a crime against their parents, the parents cannot punish that person at the same level they would with others because of emotional bondage. If there were no emotion, how long could this person hold on to the thought, "The child's survival is what my survival is? We live in this world through children"?

Our survival mechanisms come in various forms: instincts, thoughts, intellect, feelings, and emotions. Our ability to choose these mechanisms sets us apart as the most intelligent creatures on the planet. Imagine all creatures on Earth are computers. They run through a predefined program like a snake. Only humans have access to the developer tab in their system. They can alter and update the system, ignore the existing programs, create new programs, or even wipe out everything.

3. Pranamaya Kosha – It's the vital energy, life energy.

The first two layers are of no use if you do not put the plug in energy. Electricity is also physical; it's subtle but still physical. A balance in prana, or energy, leads to physical and psychological balance. The state of our prana determines our overall health, so Ayurveda, Japanese, and Chinese medicines and therapies focus on balancing prana rather than treating the physical body. Prana is considered a subtle or Shookshma body. When prana is in control, our psychological state is also balanced. There are five prana vayu: Prana, Samana, Udhana, Apana, and Vyana.

Breathing in and out is our life force, known as prana. Prana also encompasses blood flow, food conversion, hunger, thirst, and energy. Experts suggest that prana development takes 6 to 10 years and recommend that children be allowed to play to facilitate this development; this is why preventing a child from playing may hinder their prana development.

The experiences in early life significantly shape a person's character, including the environment and circumstances. It's like a vending machine that dispenses different drinks randomly, and the person's response to these random occurrences is the self.

The machine offers similar things that are the worst for many people, so why does everyone come in different shapes? Why isn't everyone living in poverty turning into a thief? What is thrown at them from an early period of life is the same, like the same economic conditions and similar problems, but their response to them is different. Could this responding nature also be karma? Where does it come from? Some say it's genes, but it's not a guaranteed answer. Then, there must be something that comes before a person is born. Yes, it is karma, which goes back to a previous life. Then how does this nature exist without a physical body to carry forward the memory?

CHAPTER 4

NON BIOLOGICAL SELF

A large fish swims in a circular pattern in the ocean. It moved so fast in a circular pattern that it created a vortex in the center. After some time, the fish died, and its body left the vortex. However, the water continued to move in the same circular pattern until its energy dissipated and became part of the ocean. When the fish died and the vortex was still active, another fish's egg was swept into the vortex by the force of the water. The egg transformed into a small fish and eventually evolved into a big fish. This fish also moves in the same circular pattern as the previous fish, continuing the vortex. The fish believed that the circular pattern was a part of itself, and if it moved out of it, it wouldn't be the same fish. If we say that the fish that died earlier took another life as this new fish because both rotate in the same circular pattern and the force of water and the pattern in which it is moving is the soul of the fish, would it be correct? It's a simplified way of saying.

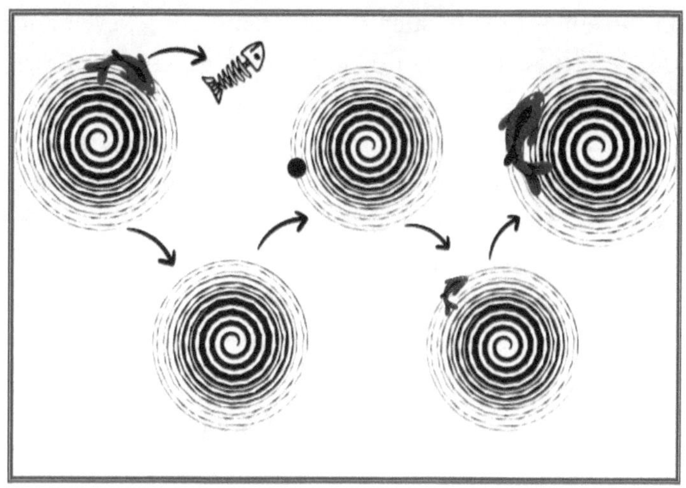

Illustration 2

After 50 years of schooling, you may forget your friend's name, where they came from, their face, and other features, but you remember thinking that there used to be a person who behaved in a certain way and had a particular nature. This nature differs from remembering a name, appearance, and where they come from. You have a repetitive habit of eating a specific food. You have a repetitive habit of reacting to certain things and situations in particular ways that only you do. Some of this repetitive nature continues its journey even after death, just like the vortex after the fish died.

What you consider yourself is the memory of a certain repetitiveness; much repetition dies with death, like their physical body and name. However, some patterns remain in the environment, such as nature and desire, even after death. If these patterns find expression, we say it's another life. However, if all the memory and repetition go away but you remain in the same place where you are, then we say you have attained Samadhi. Even if you are as large as a one-mile vortex, you are still tiny compared to the ocean. The fish, vortex, and waves are small creations in the sea. If the fish do not succumb to any forces, slow down, and stay in one place, not giving any scope to any repetition, then the vortex and the waves disappear. The water is as still as a stone, so you have become one with the ocean. Now, if this fish dies, nothing will remain to continue its journey in circles; this is where yogis aspire to reach.

There are two ways of looking at it:

1. Shoonyaka (Nothingness, the Buddhist way) - the vortex disappears and ceases to exist.

2. Poornaka (Completeness) - the vortex disappears, but it is still a part of the same ocean water that creates the waves. Once it loses its identity as the vortex, it becomes the ocean.

Researchers have conducted experiments on water and stated that it can hold memory. Water's chemical arrangement may not change, but it can cause a different psychological effect based on what it is exposed to. For example, a man experimented on plants, planting two saplings in pots. He labeled one pot "Good" and the other "Evil" and placed them in a visible location. After two weeks, the plant in the "Good" pot flourished beautifully, while the plant in the "Evil" pot almost died. This demonstrates the potential effect that exposing water to different conditions can have on living organisms.

If you take some water and stare at it with intense emotion for some time, the water carries the same memory. When you consider your body, mind, and emotional memory as yourself, and when you give the water your emotion by staring at it intensely, you transmit the emotional memory to the water outside. This means you are not only inside but also outside and away from your body. Who you are is a distinct memory; certain types of memory die when the body dies. However, other types of memory live outside of the body after death. These memories take on new life in a new body. The body occupies some space in the universe; it disassembles into atoms when it dies. The other memory that is a part of who you are is also part of the universe; those memories are also held by the universe. The other memory is subtle and in a different dimension; viewing it with normal senses is difficult.

Soul or Atman are just names we have given to that part of us that continues its journey even after our death. So whatever the soul is, it continues its journey, but where does it go, and how do you know? Once a person dies, the soul or Atman does not have any sense or control. It has some nature, and based on that nature, it desires certain things and pursues its desires in its next life. There were many sayings in old times about past life and future life. In the Buddhist tradition, it is said that if a man is wild and cruel, like an animal or even worse, then he is most likely to take life as a wild animal because that suits, or we say it is very similar to his nature, not because it is a punishment from any god.

Erasing all memories has been the highest priority in this culture.

Please refer to the diagram below, which depicts a being with different layers of memory represented by circles. The outermost layer represents the body, while the inner circles represent the mind, prana, Vignamaya, and anandamaya. Only the outer circle (i.e., the body) gets erased when a person dies. The inner circles remain intact, forming a new outer circle based on the innermost circle. Saints who practice yoga kriyas can consciously erase all the inner circles until only the body remains. Eventually, when the body dies, the outer circle is also erased. Now, nothing remains inside to continue the journey. This is what we refer to as moksha, mukthi, or Jeevasamadhi. This is the ultimate freedom from the cycle of life and death.

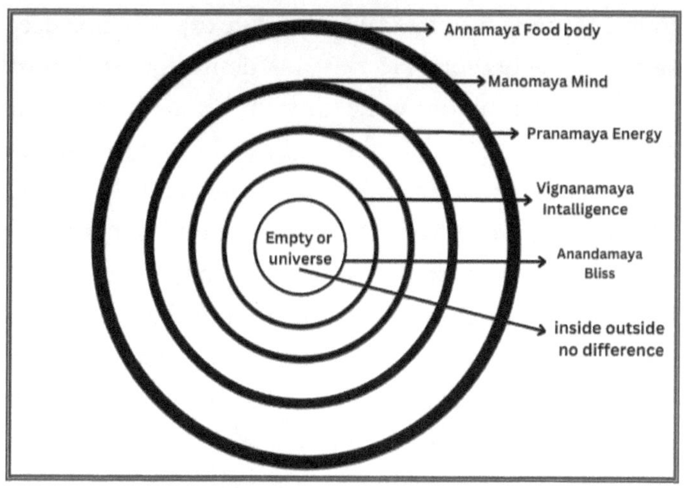

Illustration 3

Some people lose their sense of time in meditation because they withdraw their attention from their senses. The mind and body have internal cycles like sleep, eating, and reproduction. These cycles draw our awareness outward toward our physical form. You enter a deep meditative state when you can direct your attention inward and focus solely on the self. However, once the cycle time arrives, our consciousness is again pulled outward toward our body and mind, preventing us from achieving Samadhi. To reach Samadhi, one must break free from these cycles. When people attain Maha Samadhi, they are no longer bound to these cycles and are no longer conscious of the date and time.

Ramakrishna Paramahansa is a well-known spiritual leader, and his life story includes an interesting approach to maintaining his physical body while experiencing deep states of meditation. He kept his desire for food alive, which allowed him to wake up from his meditative state once the cycle time arrived. This helped him maintain his body's natural cycle and prevented him from falling into a permanent state of Samadhi. He broke his last cycle after completing his work, and after three days of not eating, he achieved Nirvikalpa Samadhi, a state where even food cannot bring him to the physical body. "Vikalpa" means options, and "nirvikalpa" refers to having no options. The concept of Samsara is like a circle, while Sannyasa is like a straight line. A straight line has a clear beginning and ending, but a circle has no end. The end here is not of consciousness; it's eternal.

Another example.

King Yudhishtara, from the times of Mahabharat, went to heaven after performing rigorous yoga practices. Surprisingly, he found his cousin Dhuryodhana there, which made him feel bad—and filled with anguish. Yudhishtara pondered why his brothers and wife, who had followed their dharma and been good, had not attained a place in heaven while Dhuryodhana did. After much contemplation, he realized that he was still holding onto his hatred for Dhuryodhana, the last string holding him back. Although he had let go of his family, kingdom, and love relationships, he couldn't let go of his enmity towards Dhuryodhana. So, he did sadhana, finally released his hatred, and attained samadhi.

Flow of Life process

According to the theory of evolution in science, life first originated in water as bacteria. Later, these bacteria evolved into many aquatic creatures, amphibians, and animals, eventually leading to humans. Bacteria, to humans, represent biological evolution, where a biological memory multiplies itself and transforms into a more complex form of biological memory. The other memories that exist outside the body after death evolve similarly, although they do not go through all the creatures. As a biological being, you evolved over millions of years; similarly, what you are as a non-biological being evolved after many lifetimes spent living as various creatures. You did what needed to be done as that creature to meet its survival needs. The experience as that creature imprinted some memory into the non-biological you. In this way, your non-biological memory multiplies itself, transforms into a complex form, and takes life as a different creature in its next lifetime, often as a higher conscious creature. Refer to illustration 4 below.

A rock or a lump of mud does not have life; they don't protect themselves. There is no concept of existence and non-existence for them. An earthworm has life, but it may not know it exists. A dog knows it exists; it has emotions and feelings to some extent. A human possesses a higher level of consciousness and understands his existence on a different level than any other creature.

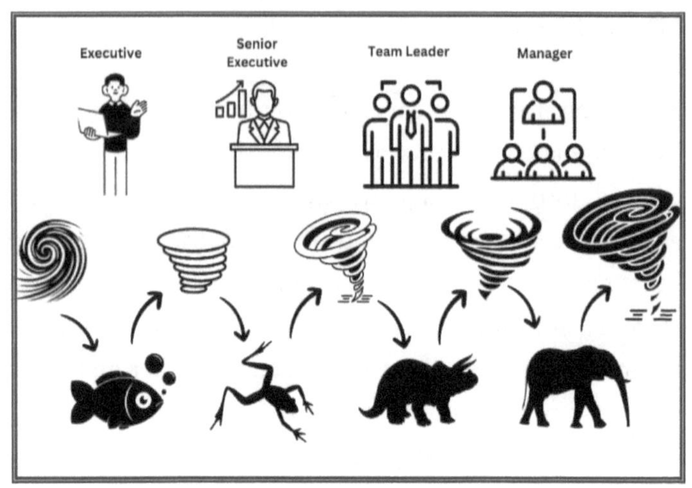

Illustration 4

Analogy: - We improve and learn new skills as we switch jobs and adapt to different work environments. The adaptation process goes deep and leaves an impression that we tend to think from that perspective even after leaving that job. The memory of work experience is also part of us, shaping our perspectives. Similarly, living as a different creature puts some memories and experiences into the nonbiological self, so in its next life, it takes life as an upgraded, higher-conscious creature. However, there are also beliefs that karma may cause one to revert to evolution, becoming stuck at a certain point.

***

This Non Biological self is referred as Vignamaya kosh - (Vishesh or Vivek gyan – extraordinary, puzzle solving)

The transitory body lies between the physical body and the subtle body, which the five senses cannot perceive. However, you can perceive it in a different form. The physical body cannot exist without the subtle body. First, a subtle body is born, leading to the creation of the physical body. Before creating anything, we imagine it and then bring it into existence. When you watch a movie, your understanding of it is called vignamaya. When you read something, you understand it with vignanamaya, which comprises various aspects.

- Memory
- Longsight into events
- Intellect
- Collection of information.
- Logical reasoning
- Testing abilities.
- Analytical
- Imagination

Meditation, resilience, reading, and debates are good for the vignanamaya kosha.

Viveka doesn't exist in Emotion. It requires a different education system.

5. Anandamaya kosha.

In the state of deep sleep, one loses awareness of the physical body, and in the absence of dreams, there exists a profound emptiness that is Anandamaya, characterized by the absence of intellect, agency, and personal identity. This profound state of restfulness is anandamaya. Letting go of Ahankara allows Anandamay to emerge. Music, art, and a good environment are essential for its growth. God and deities can guide you to anandamaya, but to progress, you must move beyond the deities.

CHAPTER 4.1. PRARABDH, SANCHITTA AND BRAHMAN.

PRARABDHA: Those strong waves from the vortex that cannot be ignored or avoided. Pra Arabdham means that which has already begun and is currently being done. It's a released arrow; the arrow should hit someone or fall but cannot be brought back to the bow in the same way. Prarabdha cannot be avoided or changed; it can only be exhausted by experiencing. Meaning used up thoroughly. For example, the Kshatriya within Arjuna must be exhausted to move further to Brahman, or else the Kshatriya within Arjuna will interfere in the path of Brahman. Experiencing is the only way you can fulfill the purpose and move further. You cannot turn against yourself. Prarabdha is that part of memory within you that makes you the person you are. It includes your talents, capabilities, fears, and anxieties. Those results of past actions give birth to the present body.

In a particular movie, a man lives in a dream with his wife, who died years ago. She is not real but a projection of his mind, yet he spends ten years in this dream with her. The movie's director explains that there is a different reality for everyone, and for this man, his wife is real. He must live with her even knowing she is not real because she has been troubling him for a long time, and ignoring or trying to forget about her is impossible. He must live that dream to leave it.

Similarly, in the Hindu epic Mahabharata, the warrior Arjuna is in a dream of Kshatriya. He knows there is a higher reality, such as liberation, after Krishna shows him Vishwaroopam. However, he has to live this dream as a Kshatriya. If he takes the path to liberation without performing his duties, the Kshatriya within him will not let him move further. On the path to liberation as a monk, one has to beg for food. If someone insults him during this process, the Kshatriya within him will not let him let it go. Therefore, to leave the Kshatriya string, he must live that string. Without living it, he is held as a reason for political imbalance, and many depend on him as the Kshatriya king. This also causes him karma.

Sanchitham purva sambandhamu

Everything you do and abstain from with will is karma. This karma creates waves; some refer to them as seeds. Prarabdha is the manifestation of those seeds that have sprouted in this life, which you are experiencing now. Sanchitta is the collection of karma that exists in the form of seeds and is waiting to manifest. As they say, "a packed seed dies by the Fire of knowledge," like a farmer who kept a bag of seeds for next year's crop, and those seeds are roasted in a fire; now there are no more seeds, it's done. Even if you try cultivating that burnt seed, it cannot spring to life; that's why advythas pravachan is needed; it's like Fire that burns the seeds of upcoming karma. If Advyatha Vedanta digests, you can stop upcoming karma, but prerabdha has already started; you must experience it. Sanchita is like the overall vortex. Prarabdha is like the most dominant waveform vortex, which is visible on top.

Sanchitta doesn't come into play in this life. You can practice yoga and meditation to eliminate Sanchitta, but you must still experience prarabdha. Once you remove the sense of doership, Sanchitta is no more.

A person feels he has lost his childhood and wishes to relive it again. Losing childhood could be prarabdha or coincidence, but when experiencing prarabdha, he drops a new seed by wishing to relive childhood. A person is affected by someone, and while experiencing this, drops new seeds into sanchitta by wishing for revenge. However, an enlightened person merely submits his body to the operation of prarabdha karma. So, sanchitta goes by gyanagni (the fire of knowledge) and sadhana, while prarabdha is experienced, and they attain Samadhi. It's important to understand that there is no other way to achieve it, and even great sages like Ramana Maharshi and Rama Krishna Paramahansa suffered from diseases like cancer. Mahatmas, or great souls, accept their prarabdha karma, even if it entails suffering. They may have to return to bear it if they don't choose to experience it. Those who remain equanimous while bearing their prarabdha, whether good or bad, do not plant new seeds and don't shoot more arrows, but finish the released arrow decently. You cannot escape; you witness it without creating new karma.

Misconceptions of Brahman or Samadhi

Remembering past life, witnessing the soul leaving the body, and feeling energy surge through their spine and hit the top of their skull. Some see experiences like these, which normal people consider supernatural, as enlightenment. All those things can make people aware that there is more to life than they previously knew. During meditation, one can become aware of oneself as pure consciousness radiating through one's body and mind. By focusing on their breath, one can slow down the activity of their mind, leading to moments of stillness, where the mind is shut down, and they are not sleeping. There is something awake watching, where they can experience true reality, also known as Brahman.

As per Adi Shankara Acharya, you should never do Kundalini Yoga. While awakening Kundalini, you will undergo various supernatural experiences; you may gain some control over some of them. Some people perceive these experiences as exceptional abilities, and they become lost in these abilities, causing their striving for liberation to end. Unfortunately, most people seek enlightenment because life is suffering, and they cannot solve their problems. They see enlightenment as a solution to all their problems, and now they have these special abilities, which undermines the reason for seeking enlightenment. They will wander outside for some time with their new talents, but they will eventually seek enlightenment. Just like money, relationships, and power, we become attached. You could become attached to your abilities, too. In ancient times, during the Satya Yuga and Treta Yuga, it was common to have abilities that are now considered highly supernatural, but even then, having such skills was not regarded as enlightenment. When you withdraw your attention from everything you consider yourself, you should be dead or at least asleep, but you are more awake than usual. That awareness is what we refer to as Brahman. As some masters have said, "You don't have to do anything. You are already Brahman. You have to dispel the ignorance that you are not Brahman."

Erasing the boundaries is different from what it seems. It's in layers and layers. On the path to Brahman, there are various types of strings. Some people say they are chakras, energy points. These strings are barriers to the Samadhi.

1. Survival string: Fear is a string—if one can't let go of the fear of survival and cannot live a fulfilling life, enlightenment is a far way off. Food and sleep are dominant factors in life. Food comes from Earth, so it is highly connected with Earth. Gautama Buddha did sadhana to overcome his basic instincts by fasting, which reflects the element of Earth and the inability to trust nature.

2. Pleasure strings—A pleasure seeker desires to experience the world more intensely, but feelings of guilt can hinder this desire. Guilt can lead to mood swings, relationship problems, and mental disharmony. When an individual fails to meet their own expectations, they may feel that something is wrong with them. Additionally, constantly comparing oneself to others and not accepting oneself for who they are can also lead to feelings of guilt.

3. Willpower – Willpower is blocked by shame—the biggest disappointment in oneself. The fire chakra is responsible for our prestige and the need to maintain our image. If it is blocked, it can lead to a victim mentality with constant complaints about the world, which can also result in stomach anxiety. This can cause a lack of self-respect and self-loathing, leading to repressed anger. If the fire chakra functions well, it empowers us with wisdom and strength. People with a well-functioning fire chakra are doers, like businesspeople or politicians.

4. Heart .

   Heart chakra influences artists who want to engage in creative endeavors and seek more intense experiences in life than business people. It is often blocked by grief.

   Below this point, all are for survival and self-preservation; above this point, you have longings to go beyond. This position occupies a central space and presents numerous opportunities; however, it may also prove challenging to navigate and derive meaningful outcomes from such an option.

5. Sound or truth. We may have difficulty speaking the truth or expressing ourselves, feel judged for what we say, and be out of touch with who we are. We may also withhold and swallow. It's a power center where enormously influential people have balanced sound chakras. It is blocked by lies.

6. Vision Insight

    Until this point, one can only see physical reality. From here, one sees everything clearly the way it is. The cognitive faculties of the mind consist of mental images and abstract ideas.

7. Pure Consciousness: it is blocked by attachments. One must let go of all kinds of attachments.

    Some of us have this question: These repetitivenesses are what we are; otherwise, we wouldn't exist; it's shoonyaka nothingness.

Imagine the body, mind, and emotions as electrical objects like televisions, air conditioners, and light bulbs. They all require electricity to function and come to life when you turn them on. The light bulb illuminates the room, the air conditioner cools the air, and the television shows images and sounds. They stop functioning when you turn them off, but the electricity remains. Suppose the bulb, air conditioner, and television take automatic repetitive action tendencies. Without your intervention, the bulb lights up at a particular time and switches off at another time, so you may think the light bulb is everything by itself and that there couldn't be any source to it. This ignorance needs to be dispelled to realize Brahman.

Similarly, we often consider our body, mind, and emotions as everything, forgetting that there is a source. Returning attention from all the senses is like switching off all the lights, television, and air conditioners, but the electricity exists. Something exists even after retrieving our attention from all the senses and self-centeredness. Just like the electricity that powers our electrical objects, something brings forth the body and mind.

Suppose we go deep into these cycles biologically. When we inhabit a human body, our body produces different pleasure hormones: serotonin, oxytocin, endorphins, and dopamine. Oxytocin is released when we engage in activities like falling in love, getting married, or giving birth. The pleasure we experience from these activities makes us pursue them because nature wants us to continue our journey into the future and survive. If there were no pleasure, many would see it as an unnecessary responsibility. So nature tricks us with these pleasures. Animals, however, are bound to their survival instincts without any leverage or choice. Dopamine is another hormone released when we achieve something significant or successful. This is another way that nature ensures survival. Wise leaders who guide the masses toward positive outcomes also contribute to their species' survival. Each of these hormones plays a role in ensuring our survival and continuation as a species.

If Memory is what you are, your child is also you, and your student is also you. Even if there is massive development in artificial intelligence, a machine holds your entire Memory of all dimensions. Still, you will remain where you are. That machine couldn't be you; it could be a re-creation of you, which does the same repetitive things.

When you sleep and wake up, you would not wake up in the artificial intelligence creation just because it is the same Memory. You would be in the same place. Even if there are 1,000 reactions of the same Memory, you would still see the world from your body and wouldn't wake up in another's. This clearly states that there is something in us that is not any memory.

Once you realize that you are not just your body, mind, emotions, and memory, you become aware of the true self within you. Only with memory can you distinguish oneness or separation, whether it is the same or different memory, whether it is an apple or an orange. That which is not any form of memory you cannot distinguish. The consciousness you cannot distinguish. When you completely dispel ignorance, the memory of what remains awake cannot be distinguished from any other living creature, whether it is Mr. A, Mr. B, or any other being. This state of being without any identities is what we call brahman.

CHAPTER 5

DHARMA CODE OF CONDUCT

Understanding dharma and its reasoning will help us understand how we can draft a code of conduct for ourselves.

Dharma differs based on various aspects and is sometimes complementary to others. Dhr means to uphold, support, and sustain. Dharma is that which helps in sustaining social, political, and economic order while nurturing inner nature.

I.   Dharma of a thing;

Burning is fire's dharma, and floating is water's dharma. The essence of a thing defines it, and without that, it loses its identity; this is the dharma of a thing. Similarly, a man should take his dharma based on his nature. The nature of a man is fundamental, and the code of conduct he sets for himself to sustain that nature is his dharma. Also, dharma helps the created universe. Nature is created based on his past karma, and the code of conduct that allows for the created nature is dharma, which is drafted considering moral, legal, and social elements. Thus, he can sustain himself with nature, but at the same time, he is maintaining ecological balance.

Those strong waves from the vortex that you cannot stop—you cannot move against them; you have to move along with them. Moving along with them is the only way to slow them down and stop one day. In the same way, a person's nature is like those strong waves, desiring certain things that cannot be suppressed or overthrown. Based on this inner nature, one should follow their dharma, which is not against the inner self. The code of conduct of that dharma is drafted considering the social, economic, and political aspects of the times, so it creates ecological balance. By living as a Kshatriya, one can leave the Kshatriya string, bringing balance to the universe. As gurus say, no one can avoid prarabdha; it can only be exhausted by experiencing it. To exhaust the prarabdha decently, one needs a code of conduct called dharma.

Some psychologists believe that certain urges of a man cannot be controlled; they can only be focused. You can channel them in a positive direction. The whole system of marriage and life partners is based on the idea that humans have specific needs, and to address these needs decently, we need a system; otherwise, it will be a complete mess. Similarly, a man's nature requires a particular framework to express itself respectably. If there is no system, it will try to find its expression in any way possible.

II.   Swadharma / Verna dharma.

Each part of the social mechanism is as important as the other. Each Verna is described as a limb of society, serving a unique purpose. You choose that part of society based on your nature. Verna dharma is the function of a group of people who share a similar nature. Dharma encompasses the duties of a member of society. All have specific responsibilities, and performing those duties to sustain the structure of society is what dharma entails. It involves maintaining one's inner nature while nurturing social development.

Type of people with respective work and skills

In bhagavath geetha chapter 4:13

chatur-varnyam maya srstam
guna-karma-vibhagasah
tasya kartaram api mam
viddhy akartaram avyayam

According to the three modes of material nature, the work described to them, and the four divisions of human society were created. Although I am the creator of this system, I know that I am still the non-doer, being unchangeable. Education helps to understand a person's nature; based on this nature, they go to the respective varna. That which supports the existing is dharma.

Swadharma: even with imperfection, follow your dharma rather than perfectly following others' dharma.

III. Dharma as Duties and Moral Pursuit of a Man (Dharma, Artha, Kama, and Moksha)

- *Dharma:* . Dharma includes duties, rights, laws, conduct, and moral values. Dharma enables social order and virtuous conduct: duties and ethical pursuit of a man.

- *Artha:* Economy, prosperity, and Means of life. Artha refers to pursuing material wealth to support oneself and one's family. It encompasses all the activities and resources that enable an individual to achieve a desired state of being. Artha includes wealth, career, and activities to make a living with financial and economic prosperity, which will enable one to pursue other remaining pursuits.

- *Kama:* Kama encompasses pleasure, love, and psychological values. It encompasses desires, wishes, passions, emotions, and pleasures of the senses. In other words, the aesthetic enjoyment of life, affection, and love—with or without sexual connotations—comprise Karma.

- *Moksha:* Liberation from the cycle of life, death, and rebirth. Cultivating virtuous values through meditation forms the basis of Moksha.

Considering what dharma is in different situations, we must adapt to different meanings.

1. Brahmana dharma

Nature of Brahman: Truthful good hold on sense. Satvika character. Sincerity and self-restraint, forgiveness, knowledge, and wisdom.

Pursuit of Brahmana: The person seeking liberation involves himself in all sorts of activities that help him lead to liberation. Whether through bhakti, the study of Vedanta, or performing serious austerities and meditation, everything may be optional, but a man wants to use every possible source available. Everyone may be seeking liberation, but this man is at a different level and is involved in various aspects related to it. A Brahmin pursues no identity or universe as identity.

Brahmins who taught kshatriyas using (astra) weapons, why didn't they use the same when there was a problem in their work? It is because they pursue no identity and desire to lose all strings. If they try to protect themselves, they are not dropping the strings but holding on to them.

Duties and responsibilities of Brahmins: They study and teach the Vedas and perform serious austerities. Guiding and sacrifices are Brahmin duties. Brahmins work as intermediaries between God and ordinary people, acting as a bridge between the universe as an identity and a limited identity. Thus, they can guide limited identity toward ultimate identity. They spread spiritual knowledge.

Why is Brahman depicted as the head on top? Even Kshatriyas have to listen to Brahman. Refer to Illustration 1 in Chapter 2, where the circle of Brahman, with erased boundaries, sees everyone within him and seeks everyone's well-being. That's why, many times, there were changes in rulers, but the Brahmanas were treated as they should be. Brahman has the universe as their identity, not a particular kingdom, so everything he says considers the well-being of all creatures in the universe. There is a system that leads people to enlightenment, and enlightened masters teach this system. Under the guidance of masters, Kshatriyas built and protected the system.

2. Nature of Kshatriya: Bravery, brilliance, courage, not running away from battle, and generosity. A Kshatriya goes to heaven by studying the Vedas and performing the duties of dying on the battlefield—physical power.

   Pursuit of Kshatriya: You do not necessarily have to be the king of a nation; even a soldier in the army sees his identity in the entire nation, not just in protecting his family or himself. He is the one who is willing to put his life on the line for the larger entity. Kshatriya pursues a larger identity and authority over it. Pursues Glory.

Duties and responsibilities of Kshatriya: Protecting the earth by helping the good, punishing the evil and immoral, and establishing the dharma. Kshatriya's dharma involves much in implementing it, but what is dharma? The Brahmin teaches it. If the Kshatriya alone decides dharma, then it comes from a limited identity.

Why is education necessary for Kshatriyas?

The story of Ekalavya and Drona Acharya from the Mahabharata is a well-known tale in India. According to the story, Drona asks for Ekalavya's thumb as a gurudhakshina, or a token of gratitude to the teacher. However, there is a common misconception that Drona asked for Ekalavya's finger to eliminate competition and make his dearest student, Arjuna, the world's best warrior specializing in archery. In reality, as per Srimadha Bhagavatam, Ekalavya needed to learn the lesson of patience. One day, while a dog was barking on the street, Ekalavya shot four arrows at the dog's mouth, causing it to be unable to open again. It is the dog's nature to bark, but he couldn't bear it. Dronacharya saw this act and decided that Ekalavya should not possess such powers. While Ekalavya learned all about archery by keeping an idol of Dronacharya, he did not learn the other lessons that a Kshatriya should have. If Ekalavya's other qualities had been as eloquent as his archery, he would have been a Kshatriya. Drona would have let Ekalavya possess those skills. Even among Kshatriyas, not everyone was taught to use every weapon.

You might have heard this dialogue from movies: "With bigger abilities come bigger responsibilities." If anyone is unwilling or incapable of taking responsibility, we should remove their ability. Imagine a person who possesses a nuclear weapon but does not take the identity of a nation and identifies solely with his family. If something happens to his family, he is going to use the nuclear weapon. Such a person could be a danger to others. There is a tradition of aksharaabyasam, where they initiate a child for education; they say Aham brahmaasmi. Ahankara means identity, and Brahman means universe, incubating the idea that the child's identity is with the entire universe. Because the person will learn valuable skills, we use our skills to protect our identity. People may defend their identity, but that is not always good for the world. Likewise, if a person possesses the skills of Kshatriya but only has family as an identity and does everything to protect his family, it could be a disaster. That's why you should give a bigger identity with a greater set of skills, or if not possible, take away their abilities, not because they are born in a specific caste. If Ekalavya had not been impatient, Drona could have given him a bigger identity.

The profession is based on the nature of the individual, and the hierarchy one can reach in that particular work is determined by the individual's competence. In this context, competence refers to acquiring a set of skills and mastering control over one's senses, as skills are a form of power. Even among Kshatriyas, not everyone was taught to use every weapon; nowadays, we see some as soldiers, some as army generals, and some who hold control of nuclear weapons. Even now, in Kerala's martial arts, there is a unique skill called marma kala, which is only taught by the guru to those who have earned his trust and are deemed trustworthy.

Lord Hanuman received many boons from the Devas in his childhood; however, his playful nature led him to misuse his powers, and he was cursed to forget them. This was necessary, as a child should not possess such power; later, he regained his powers by being reminded of who he was.

Some people have this question: when leading beings to the ultimate is what is required of them, why don't we set everyone on the path of the ultimate? Look at some countries that follow Buddhism. What is happening there, and how are people living under foreign rule? They cannot even perform their rituals in some parts. Turning everyone into monks is not a good idea because many have not evolved to be in that space. If a Kshatriya does not do his work to save the kingdom and maintain a peaceful environment, the monks cannot do their meditation. Let the Kshatriya do his karma so he can move further, and at the same time, his work allows the monks to do their work in peace.

3. Nature of a Vyshya – Intelligence, cleverness, and creativity. Farmers, merchants, businessmen.

    Pursuit of Vyshya: Economic wealth. Prosperity of society.

    Duties and responsibilities of Vyshya: Agriculture, conducting honest trade, and breeding cattle. Ensuring the protection of crops and livestock through Krishi Goraksha is also a key responsibility, as is the production of textiles. Ultimately, Vyshya helps to maintain sufficient food availability and supports the growth and prosperity of the nation.

4. Nature Shudra- Humility, attitude of a servitor, and politeness are all qualities of a *Shudra*.

    The pursuit of Shudra: Shudra seeks a simple life and good relationships. They pursue perfection in craft or skill, doing their job well and serving others.

    The duties and responsibilities of shudra, sadhana, *and seva,* Service to the Absolute Truth, are prescribed for him. He serves God. Shudra service workers, artisans, temple creators, and temple maintenance, food, and art are Shudras.

Is Shudra any less than other varnas? No. Each one can reach the ultimate in their own way. Referring to illustration 1 from chapter 2, who is closer when you seek no identity as your goal? Kshatriyas have a bigger identity or ego; to merge with existence, they must endure many struggles. In contrast, Shudras with Seva can rapidly reduce the ego and bring about swift spiritual progress. Moreover, varna is based on nature, not birth or family lineage.

IV. Dharma as justice. Cause and effect.

Justice is a principle established by people for the systematic living of a society by its members. In a way, it represents equality or fairness. From a legal perspective, it is the protection of the law. An eye for an eye or a life for a life is not justice. One must consider various factors before rendering judgment, such as the actions of the victim before the crime was committed and the circumstances under which the perpetrator committed the crime. Being an obstacle to one's dharma is Adharma; it could have been unlawful, too.

Apadharma

Apadharma is the code of conduct for people during war or distress. Apadharma ethics of abnormal times sometimes require that the members of the Verna adapt to the duties and functions of other dharma. Why do Indian saints fight for the nation and its true identity when they realize they are beings who have attained

Brahman? Why take the nation's identity and religious identity? Because they are destroying the structure of the spiritual path laid by gurus, who are the very essence of this nation. To establish the dharma, Brahmana took on the duties of Kshatriya.

Each varna undergoes different training processes and worships different god deities to gain the ability to progress in their field. They are made with good intent, and they have their own usefulness; however, discrimination exists. In the old days, before democracy, the most cunning evil people were often in the king's administration or surroundings. From the early period of democracy, politicians were considered evil. Recently, media houses and their owners have been wicked and corrupt. Throughout history, we have seen that people with evil intentions tend to gravitate towards positions of power, authority, and wealth. Sometimes, power and authority change people's character. While social systems like the Varna system may have been created with good intentions, discrimination still exists in many forms. We see in the current world how many laws are misused.

Varna-Swadharma was considered a profession that aligned with a person's inner nature; however, over time, it became a birth-based system. The good thing is that it is gradually reverting to its original form. Recently, a significant percentage of birth-based Varna systems have become irrelevant. Previously, people followed the occupation of their parents. For instance, a person who climbed a tree for wine would do the same with his son and grandson. Similarly, people who worked as washermen and their children followed the same profession. But times have changed, and anyone can choose to work in any field. The current system emphasizes the importance of Swadharma, which means understanding one's true nature and choosing a profession that aligns with it to coexist with nature.

CHAPTER 6

CONSEQUENCES

CHAPTER 6. 1. OCCUPATION.

You might have come across this question: Should you listen to your heart or your mind?

The heart symbolizes a person's deepest desires and preferences. When we say "heart," we refer to a person's intent or quest. The heart can only tell what it wants; it desires something. The heart can only express likes and dislikes, wants and needs, and the direction it wishes to take. However, the heart cannot provide insight into how things will unfold, answer questions about possibility or consequences, or assess one's capability to handle situations. The mind handles all these calculations.

I say: you should listen to your heart in the long run and your mind in the short run. When you truly commit yourself internally to something, your mind will lay a path toward your goals. For example, if you wish to build yourself like a model, it's a 12-month journey. So, the mind will tell you what you should do daily, such as diet, workouts, and skincare routine. You should listen to your mind daily so you can transform yourself into the person you desire. However, if you listen to your heart in the short run, it wants ice cream, chocolate, and alcohol and wishes to eat and sleep. This will not bring you closer to your goal.

I would not suggest listening to your mind for long-term decisions.

If you aspire to be a creative director and make movies, it's a long-term decision. If you listen to your mind, it may bring up doubts and questions based on past experiences. It might ask if you have ever made a movie, worked as an assistant director, written a story, or have any industry connections. If you answer "no" to all these questions, your mind might perceive your goal as unattainable because it can only rely on past experiences to predict the future. The mind can only tell from its memory that what did not happen before can never occur in the future. If you listen to your intent, setting aside the possibilities, the same mind will lay a path toward your goals. How efficient the path is depends on the efficiency of the mind. In the long run, if you look to the mind as a judge, it can only judge.

"The mind is a wonderful servant but a terrible master." Krueger, A. (2017). Performing Mindful Creativity: Three South African Case Studies. https://doi.org/10.5920/pam.2017.05

Those who lack a long-term vision defined by the heart suffer in their minds because they solely rely on their intellect for guidance. The mind tries to make every situation beneficial. However, when there is no long-term goal, you do not know what is beneficial until the event has happened, and you may regret and feel resentment after the occurrence of the events. For every little thing that goes wrong, the mind will come and say that if you had done it another way, you could have avoided it. If you have a long-term goal defined by the heart, then you do not feel bad about small losses because everything you have lost serves as a step toward long-term victory.

When the heart has given your mind a direction to work in, you look up to your mind as a judge in the short run; this is beneficial. However, if the direction itself is given by the mind after calculating the possibilities, the mind may provide you with new directions now and then because it sees new possibilities as new information arrives.

The mind alone cannot accomplish anything. For instance, there is artificial intelligence: a computer fed all forms of information in the world. When someone asks a question, it answers. It performs the work if you give it a task, but the AI cannot act independently. It doesn't have its life force, nor does it have an intent of its own. If someone poses a query, it responds 100 times faster than any human, but it does not have the desire to act on its own. Some people are intelligent and have a lot of information but no direction in which to move.

They often work for someone who is not even half as intelligent as they are but has a strong intent. Some people even have these prophecies that someday artificial intelligence will become so advanced that computers will overtake the human race and enslave us because they are far more intelligent than humans. Intelligence has less to do with overtaking, but intent has more to do with overtaking us. Intelligence may aid in overtaking other people, but intelligence alone cannot overtake. It is evident from history that people with solid intent took over the world more than those with the greatest minds.

When someone fights for something that seems impossible, we say they have a heart. This means their determination is greater than the mind's calculation of the possibility of success. We say the lion's heart is not only that of a powerful creature but more than that: it embodies an uncompromising attitude, where often the mind thinks it should back down, but it doesn't.

I remember a statement from an army general about the type of cadets he wanted to recruit. He said, "Don't send those who are at the top in academics, don't send those who are at the top in sports, and don't send those with the nicest behavior. Instead, send those rebels who do not wish to surrender to anyone. We will teach them discipline." He preferred rebels because they had willpower and would fight to win over the impossible.

The mind can be trained, developed, and molded into the desired shape, whereas a person's intent or quest cannot.

Instead, it is created by pain, grief, loss, or what we call a void. We see in many individuals' lives that until they hit rock bottom, they can't set a direction and make progress in life because a strong intent sets direction and can train a person's mind to move. Often, successful people tell stories about losing someone, feeling insulted, or experiencing heartbreak at their lowest point in life, which inspires them to do something. The heart (intent) drives people to achieve something so they can become something. But often, the heart is killed by lame, unrealistic morals and a sense of being right in society. But where does this intent or quest of a person come from? Prarabdha. The feeling of void creates seeds of desires and drops them into sanchita, and that seed which sprouted in this life to find expression is prarabdha.

***

Prarabdha

Mr. A read a book yesterday. He understood the first seven chapters and then went to sleep. The book contains ten chapters in total. Today, both Mr. A and Mr. B are reading the same book. Mr. A needs to review the first seven chapters and learn the remaining three, while Mr. B has to start from the beginning. When Mr. B sees how quickly Mr. A learns the chapters, he is amazed and thinks that Mr. A must be gifted, lucky, or have some divine intervention. However, Mr. B doesn't know that Mr. A had already learned those chapters yesterday.

Even if Mr. A were to tell him, Mr. B wouldn't believe him. By "yesterday," I mean in a past life.

Some individuals possess exceptional skills in a particular field, which they have acquired in this life but learned so quickly and effortlessly that it seems extreme to others. This may seem impossible to some, but it could be due to their hard work in a previous life. In this life, they revise what they already know, and they have more new things to learn. Eventually, they excel and shine like a gem. Not necessarily; it's all about skill in a particular field. Often, people have a specific type of mindset, which can only be achieved after experiencing many life struggles. However, some people tend to have it from early life, while others look at them in amusement. Sometimes, people develop a skill or a particular mindset because of their past actions, which can lead to fruitful or challenging consequences. This is what they refer to as prarabdha. It's not only skills and talents but also fears and anxieties that we acquire as prarabdha. It is ripe for reaping.

Some people suffer in this life not just because they can't have what they want, but also because they don't believe in the continuity of life and feel envious. For example, someone could be your age, but they are far ahead in many things because of their prarabdha. Instead of taking action for what you desire, you think it is impossible and settle for something else. If unfulfilled, there is a possibility one will pursue their desires in the next life.

RAHU and KETU

If you have ever visited an astrologer or looked into astrology online, you may have encountered the concept of a Kundalini chart. Based on the alignments of the planets in the chart, astrologers determine a person's characteristics, strengths, weaknesses, desires, current position in life, and where they would like to go. The placement of Rahu and Ketu in the birth chart is significant. Rahu and Ketu are two important entities in the birth chart. Rahu is depicted as having only a head and no body, symbolizing insatiable desires because there isn't a body to digest and make it part of the self.

On the other hand, Ketu is depicted as having only a body and no head, representing influences from past experiences that affect a person's behavior and decision-making without their consciously remembering the reasons behind their actions. These influences may stem from childhood or even from past lives. Rahu indicates unfulfilled desires in the current life, while Ketu represents past experiences and their impact.

The influence of planetary position may have some validity, but not because you are born in a particular alignment; instead, it is your past karma that determines the planetary position you are born with. So gemstones and other remedies might help in this life, but the most important thing is that you must take charge of your life and deal with karma. Based on your prarabdha karma, you will have a certain nature, some existing skills, and a mindset. Prarabdha is not a fixed thing; by karma, you made it, and by doing karma, you can change it.

***

Weather and climate.

The difference between weather and climate is that weather refers to the rapid changes in the atmosphere, such as temperature fluctuations from hot to cold, which occur within seasons, days, and even hours. On the other hand, climate refers to a particular region's overall, long-term weather patterns. While the weather can vary significantly from place to place, climate represents the general atmospheric conditions of an area. It's important to note that even climate is not constant and can change over time. For example, many deserts were once oceans, and the climate of many places has evolved over thousands of years. Recently, we have been witnessing an increase in temperature year by year; the climate is also changing. (Brahmachariya, Gruhasthu, Vanaprastha, and Sanyasa are like the weather.) Changes in childhood, student life, and the early period of adult life are like weather, and a person's nature is climate. People would naturally choose fields based on their nature. One should choose the path based on the climate, not the weather. When we refer to Rahu and Ketu, we are not going for whether we are talking in view of climate, which is more constant. Understand the need that is long-term. Go with the need that is necessary in your life.

Know the essential nature of a person and set them on a sustainable development path with their existing nature. You should not choose a particular dharma simply because you were born into that family. You should not select your dharma because everyone in your surroundings expects you to be. It's like saying that just because you are born into a doctor's family, you should be a doctor and nothing else. Although you may derive most of your characteristics from your parents, there is a good percentage chance that you would make a good doctor. A huge percentage of the birth-based caste system has died. It is not just talent; you also inherit fears and anxieties from previous lives. You can suffer from your life experiences, or you can use them as a guide.

Why does everyone seek a big bungalow, a beautiful partner, fame, and influence, etc.? Is reaching that point a success?

Modern philosophers advise following your natural inclinations in life, similar to how water flows downwards. People often miss these inclinations in childhood and adolescence as they prioritize survival and social acceptance. By the time they realize their true interests, it is too late. Childhood interests are natural, not influenced by financial gain or societal recognition. Many individuals discover their passions through education, which exposes them to various opportunities. However, some may lose sight of their natural inclinations in pursuit of societal acceptance and immediate survival needs. The education system is designed to prepare individuals for current societal needs, leading many to prioritize fitting into society and meeting immediate survival needs over pursuing their true passions.

We often find ourselves drawn toward specific aspirations and goals. Still, when we compare our lives to others, we start doubting our desires and achievements, which can lead to confusion. It would be best to practice meditation and introspection. By delving deeper into our true desires and where we find fulfillment in life, we can choose a path that aligns with our aspirations. Education that equips us with the necessary knowledge and skills to pursue our chosen path can help us avoid dissatisfaction. Rather than being influenced by external factors such as someone else's wealth or luxurious lifestyle, we should focus on choosing a career that satisfies us, regardless of its financial rewards. It's important to acknowledge that economic circumstances may limit our choices.

A void created a desire, and in your journey to fulfill that desire, you have reached a point referred to as prarabdha, which means that which has already begun.

When working in a specific field for five years, you tend to develop intuition, also called pattern recognition. Sometimes, people work for more than a decade in the same field but still stumble every time something new occurs, while they find others excelling with not even half the experience they have. There are two things one could do: 1. I do not suggest this, but you realize this field is not meant for you and find where your talent lies, which means where your mind recognizes patterns easily. 2. If you have not made any journey in this field in any lifetime and still have the desire to continue in the same field, then you move with the commitment that this field may not yield anything great in this life but creates a better version of you.

CHAPTER 6.2. MORAL CODE OF CONDUCT.

By defining nature and relative occupation, you have defined yourself, what you want, and where you wish to go. With that in mind, you will want to use all resources to reach your intended goal. Sustaining and developing to a higher level means never going against your core self. For example, suppose you are a gentle and delicate person and are employed in a butcher job. In that case, it contradicts your core self, leading to personal conflict and dissatisfaction.

Spiritual leader J. Krishnamurti said, "No religion is perfect, and no culture is perfect. You cannot be under anyone's light like Buddha's or Krishna's; you must be the light yourself. Instead of conforming to a specific set of rules, define your principles. Just write your code of conduct, considering where you wish to go. I don't say do whatever you want; you may do whatever you wish, but the world will respond accordingly. Consider all other consequences while writing your code of conduct, such as legal and social. If you go too deep with nature alone and neglect the other consequences, then you may end up in jail, and even worse, it may end your life."

A nation's Constitution provides a framework for society and grants people specific rights and responsibilities. When you live in a particular country, you adhere to that nation's code of conduct. Similarly, by becoming part of a college or office, you agree to uphold that institution's specific code of conduct. However, you still have the freedom to practice your own beliefs to the extent possible. We all follow the law, and if the Constitution contradicts our code of conduct, we can use legal means to change it. Never compromise the core self.

CHAPTER 6.3. FOOD CONSEQUENCE

In Indian tradition

A bull has a robust and repetitive nature that it cannot escape, even at the cost of extreme pain. When animals eat crops on the farm, the farmers employ various methods to protect their yield, sometimes using a stick. The animals learn from their experiences, and after a few incidents, they tend to stay away from the crops, even in the absence of humans. However, a bull has a different nature. Despite being beaten, it continues to eat from the same place, seemingly unaware of the pain it causes itself. It behaves as if it is in partial sleep, not fully awake.

Hindu goddess Maa Durga is said to be killing the demon Mahisha Asura, a demon in the form of a bull. People perform severe austerities during the Navratri period to gain goddess Durga's blessings. In a way, new life springs forth by removing old karma and leaving behind the bull nature, breaking free from many cycles. As part of the rituals, one has to follow a strict diet plan.

It's like all the creatures on the planet are some computer that runs on a pre-existing program. Only humans have access to the developer tab. They can ignore some programs and write new programs, so some foods provide command over the developer tab, while some foods take away your existing control. Whether you wish to succumb to a repetitive cycle, dwell in the vortex, or come out of it.

a. Alcohol and drugs

In previous generations, street magicians used catchy phrases to attract crowds. For example, they would say, "There is a god above and an animal below, and man is in between. Above is pure consciousness, no repetitive circles and processes, and complete freedom. Below is an animal ruled by survival instincts; they repeat a predetermined program like a snake. And man is in between. He is capable of being conscious, and at the same time, he has instincts. In one's effort to fulfill life, they encounter many challenges and go through struggles and suffering where they may feel like they are suffering their consciousness. Instead of being more conscious and solving their problems, they want to kill the consciousness by consuming alcohol and other substances to escape. By consuming alcohol, the man drops below the level where he lives normally. Now, many more things are 'needs' where they used to be a choice. People don't intend to kill their consciousness, but they think it's the consciousness that is causing them suffering. There is peace in complete freedom, and there is peace in instincts, but being in between is stressful.

Once, a woman got lost in Alaska, where the temperature was -15 degrees and below. The woman slept after a long journey and couldn't feel her feet when she woke up. She rubbed her feet to warm them for walking; she suddenly felt terrible pain. At first, she tried to bear the pain, but it became unbearable for her, so she dug a small hole in the ice and buried her feet to make them numb like before. Similarly, many people dull their consciousness by consuming alcohol and drugs. Alcohol and drugs take away your control over the system.

b.   Meat.

Donating a cow (Godhana) to a Brahmin is considered highly sacred. The Brahmin seeks ultimate liberation, but to do so, he must leave behind all the repetitive strings. If he tries to abandon the food string completely, he may not survive, while other strings may remain alive, forcing him to be reborn. Therefore, to keep his body alive while he deals with other strings, he must continue eating but wishes to accumulate as little karma as possible. Unlike buffaloes and other animals, cows have a different nature. Therefore, consuming cow's milk creates less karmic debt for survival. Accumulating less karma facilitates progress on a spiritual path. Brahmins seek things that generate less karma to aid in their journey.

Consuming meat involves the suffering of animals, while plant life also experiences suffering.

The digestive system breaks down food into simpler forms, which the body absorbs. Once absorbed, the nutrients become a part of the body and contribute to its overall well-being. It is easier for the body to assimilate nutrients from green leafy vegetables than from meat. Making food a part of who you are is not only about the physical body; a being consists of five layers: physical, psychological, energy, intelligence, and bliss. The more conscious the living thing you consume, the more negative the impact will be.

By focusing on water intensely, you can transfer emotional memories to it. Similarly, an animal's emotional memory is left in its body after death. Mammals, in particular, experience intense suffering before death, leaving a lasting impression on their bodies. Consuming this distressing memory can significantly impact your non-biological memory, driving you more toward instinct than consciousness and trapping you in repetitive cycles. Some might wonder about those who ate raw meat and still thrived spiritually, like Bhakta Kannappa. I want to emphasize that while some people can ingest venom and other poisonous substances and still survive, not everyone can do the same.

Those on the spiritual path avoid onion and garlic due to their potential to stimulate certain hormones associated with rajas guna. Modern research also indicates that the consumption of onion increases testosterone in men.

It is not necessarily that you wish to reach Brahman, but life is an ever-changing journey, and you must adjust to accommodate change. So, for some time, you may want to avoid certain foods. Fasting for specific periods, known as Vrath or Dheeksha, is done so one can easily accommodate the change with the least friction. Often, it is used when making big decisions in life. It is as if you have made a decision, aiming for something significant in life, and taken a vow that until you reach that point, you will not sleep. Not literally sleep. Instead, you are conscious of every action that leads to the desired end. For example, when working on a project with a strict deadline, it is easy to get sidetracked by social media, movies, and food, only to realize that the submission date has crept up on you. To avoid this, minor changes to your eating habits can make a significant difference.

You should not eat more food than is necessary for your survival.

By consuming food, you are taking another life, whether it is from an animal or a plant. However, if you do not consume food, you are causing yourself suffering, which is also not good. Ending your life is also not a good choice because life doesn't end at death. The best thing you can do is work towards liberation, and you can choose your time and methods. You would like to accumulate as little karma as possible to reach the ultimate goal. To achieve the ultimate, you would like to accumulate as little karma as possible. However, what is necessary for an individual also varies to some extent.

Not only does the food, but the way you consume the food also impacts.

CHAPTER 6.4. LIFE PARTNER CONSEQUENCE.

In marriage, the couple promises to help each other in all four pursuits of life: Dharma, Artha, Kama, and Moksha. People marry because they have different physical, emotional, and psychological needs. These needs should not come in the spiritual path. Does your need fulfillment take you away from where you want to go or aid you? Nowadays, people are marrying those with a similar interest in their future lives.

If you go to the ocean, you need a ship; if you are climbing a mountain, your needs are different. If you are going to jingle, your needs are different. As you pack your bag according to your destination, choose your companions wisely for the journey ahead.

Varna is not determined by birth but by an individual's nature, ambitions, and vision for life. Therefore, you should choose your work and lead a life based on your nature. Similarly, you should choose your life partner based on these principles. Relationships are seen as a means to reach a common destination. So, it would help if you surround yourself with people who have similar aspirations. A relationship cannot thrive if you are moving in different directions. It won't be easy to make peace within if you have chosen a partner to accompany you in artha and kama but not dharma.

CHAPTER 6.5. TYPE OF YOGA CONSEQUENCE.

The type of yoga you adapt is of consequence. All the yogas have some problems following alone, so you should follow all to some extent. Four categories of yoga can help you reach the ultimate: 1) Bhakti Yoga, 2) Gyana Yoga (Adyatha Vedanta), 3) Karma Yoga, and 4) Kriya Yoga. Sanatana Dharma's varna system is based on Karma Yoga. You have to do some karma, even if you may be a Gyana or Bhakti yogi. All other yogas are something you choose, whereas karma is inevitable. Everyone does it. So, based on patterns of karma and sequencing, people have installed this complex system.

a.   Gyana Yoga

As long as you have questions, you cannot fully engage in meditation. Therefore, start with reasoning in Vedanta and then progress to other processes. However, for some, Vedanta alone suffices. This form of yoga is vital, particularly in the modern world, which highly values reasoning.

If ignorance is the problem, the solution is knowledge.

Knowing can happen only when you are open to perception. People in your surroundings often say beautiful things, but they bounce off your head because you are not seeking. Seeking means having the eagerness to know the answers to your questions. With knowledge, you can save yourself from falling into repetitive patterns. Knowing and detachment are two different things. In one case, only intellectual knowing occurs, and one who has not practiced detachment can become arrogant about their perceived knowledge.

b. Bhakti Yoga,

If desires are the problem that creates loops, then transferring the desire toward God is the way of a bhakti yogi.

You may be a scholar in Vedanta who understands Brahman intellectually, but bhakti will enhance the awareness of Brahman. A devotee will have the vision of God at the time of enlightenment. Many have this vision of Ganesha, Kali, and Shiva. The form of God is a powerful source of bhakti.

Pursuing enlightenment could also be considered a desire; ultimately, one must let go of all attachments. The Bhakti Yogi leaves all attachments by keeping God in the highest position, and one fine day, he must leave God. The bhakti way is the easiest way to reach Samadhi. Some have even suggested that even when in the presence of God, one should continue to progress. In this belief system, God is not the ultimate goal; Samadhi is, and Samadhi means oneness with the universe. Sometimes, the deities you worship can guide you toward the desired state. Keep advancing in your spiritual practice.

Belief and disbelief.

We all have some level of logical reasoning. Before believing anything, we typically use our logical reasoning to question it. Once we receive satisfactory reasoning, we believe. Belief is like standing on a table. The legs or pillars of the table represent the reasons behind our beliefs, explaining why we think they are true. When we understand the reasoning behind someone else's belief, we can use our reasoning to show them how weak or flawed their reasoning is. Instead of unquestioningly believing, people should question and analyze how their beliefs align with their logical reasoning. By metaphorically breaking the legs of the table one by one, we create fear and anxiety in the person standing on the table, as they feel like they are about to fall. You experience a similar feeling when someone is breaking the reasoning behind your belief, as if you are about to fall off something.

There is a simple person who believes in God and has his reasons for doing so. There is an atheist who can never believe in God, and debates with this man successfully convince him to become an atheist by providing better reasoning. However, the atheist doesn't believe in God, and there is some logical reasoning. There is a sage-like being who debates with this atheist, cracks the reasoning behind this atheist philosophy, and converts him into a theist. If you go by intellect, every time you believe and disbelieve, someone would come up with more logical reasoning. So, your belief changes whenever someone presents a new question. Bhakti yoga and Gyana yoga can have this problem; for them, Karma and Kriya yoga can provide a solution.

c.   Karma Yoga

You can choose other yogas like raja yoga, jnana yoga, and bhakti yoga, but there is no question of choosing karma yoga as it is inevitable. Karma yoga alone brings yoga directly to life. Karma yoga is not about what is done; instead, it is about how it's done; everything can be spiritualized. For your well-being and to bring welfare to the world, choose a work that aligns with your inner self. You will have less resistance toward the work and should never do anything against your conscience. Selfishness is the problem that entangles us in strings. Purposeful but unselfish work is the solution.

"Do it, but unselfishly. Distance yourself from the doership. You are not the doer; watch it from a third man's perspective." Sentences like these made me crazy once. If you say you are a doer, you are giving energy to the vortex. You are providing energy to repetitive strings; the goal is to eliminate all strings. Some strings you can ignore, and some strings you cannot, so you are involved in those strings that cannot be ignored, so they don't bother you anymore. Watching from the third person's perspective is referred to as Thuriya.

Accepting excellent and bad in life with the same spirit. In karma yoga, the focus is not on what you receive in return. Instead, it's about recognizing and breaking free from the repetitive patterns in your actions, leading to a path of liberation. This realization serves as a crucial preparatory step. While abruptly opposing these patterns may not be beneficial, introducing subtle changes will eventually lead to their cessation.

d. Raja Yoga – Path of Experience

A wandering mind is the issue; raja yoga changes it into a concentrated mind.

You know it's real only when you experience it. The realization is not meant for psychological understanding alone; instead, it is to be experienced.

Why You Should Be Meditative (Raja Yoga), Even If You Are Not Seeking Liberation

When you join a new job, you struggle for the first few days. Even if you work in the same field and do similar tasks, your mind may feel hyperactive and struggle to adjust to the new environment, making circles, patterns, and repetitiveness of work. After a few days, your mind begins to create mental models of the processes, and once it recognizes patterns and repetition, it becomes at ease. During this adjustment period, you may experience a heightened sense of alertness and awareness, or increased consciousness. Your mind is in the process of identifying and adapting to the new, long-term daily routines and repetitive processes. This heightened consciousness is a natural response to a completely new situation where your usual ways of thinking and doing things may not apply.

People often solidify their character based on time and situation. However, what was once beneficial can become uncomfortable and unsuitable, itching like a thong for themselves and others. It's important to recognize when it's time to change, but change is incredibly difficult for some. When they tried to change by force, they broke into pieces. Think of character as a metal object and consciousness as the fire or heat that shapes and molds it.

Developing a consistent meditation practice can assist in clearing karma and enhancing your ability to absorb new knowledge effortlessly. This leads to improved learning experiences, as past karma no longer hinders your progress.

Science has less to do with reality and more to do with repetitiveness.

According to science, it cannot be considered valid if you do something that defies scientific explanation. Even if you accomplish it once, it cannot be replicated, and science does not recognize it as valid. For example, consider the formula A+B whole square; whether you use it once or a million times, you always get the same result, and science accepts it. This shows that existing science values repetition over reality because that makes it scientific. Science is valuable as it provides consistent results, ensuring certainty. However, the Western or European approach to science, primarily focused on the physical and chemical aspects, may not be the only valid form of science when dealing with spirituality. We may be unaware of many other types of science due to our current perceptions. Various yoga methods and processes can lead to enlightenment, and no single method suits everyone. Often, enlightened individuals tailor a unique mantra or specific yoga practice for each person. It is not appropriate to rationalize these sciences based on conventional scientific norms.

CHAPTER 6.6. THE GOD YOU WORSHIP IS A CONSEQUENCE.

a.   Goddess Saraswati and Lakshmi.

Shiksha and Vidya are different. Shiksha encompasses the understanding of the physical realm, including disciplines such as mathematics, chemistry, biology, essential life skills, and various artistic expressions. Shiksha is necessary; at the same time, it might position the individual as an external observer, seeking to learn methods to optimize their interaction with the world. In contrast, Vidya fosters the awareness of one's intrinsic connection to the world, emphasizing that individuals are not isolated entities. Vidya imparts lessons on Dharma, Justice, and elevated spiritual wisdom. While Shiksha may cultivate a sense of Ahankara, or ego, Vidya encourages humility. The Goddess Saraswati is revered for bestowing both Shiksha and Vidya upon individuals. She symbolizes the elegance of knowledge and wisdom. Where Saraswati is present, there follows Lakshmi, the power of wealth.

Lakshmi symbolizes wealth; wealth is a manifestation of energy. While money itself is merely a physical medium, the intrinsic value it represents is rooted in energy, enabling various possibilities for its use. If Goddess Saraswati gives us knowledge that can bring wealth, why do we still worship Goddess Lakshmi?

Some individuals believe that their intelligence is the cause of their suffering. They think that if they were less smart, they would be happier. There are various reasons for this belief, but a key one is that if there is too much knowledge and no energy to act on the knowledge they have, they remain bitter about their potential.

"The way the world works, you don't get gifts without a corresponding temptation." - Jordan Peterson.

Just having knowledge and being smart doesn't mean the world will automatically favor you. The world values your ability to use that knowledge effectively. Knowledge or skill by itself isn't sufficient; to move forward in life, you need the energy that drives wealth creation. It's similar to saying that with the internet providing endless information, everyone should be a wealthy entrepreneur. However, it takes effort and energy to act and make things happen, which is when the universe responds. People pray to goddess Lakshmi, as she represents energy and abundance.

If a person has little to no knowledge (Shiksha), they must put in a lot of energy to regain energy (wealth). On the other hand, someone with a lot of knowledge but no effort will not gain anything. A wealthy person without knowledge may eventually lose their wealth. While spirituality is greater wealth, the support of the sustenance God Lakshmi is also needed. Without some knowledge, wealth is hard to achieve, and without experiencing wealth, it can be tough to understand higher spiritual knowledge, like Vidya, which guides one towards moksha. Therefore, Goddess Saraswati and Goddess Lakshmi are essential for a fulfilling life.

b.   Lord Ganesha

The word "Vigna" means obstacle, and "Vigneshwara" means someone who removes all obstacles in life. Due to his large head, which represents intelligence, Lord Ganesha could see all possible outcomes, enabling him to navigate through his problems. This is why, when someone starts something new, the first thing they do is go to Ganesh Puja. Before beginning yajna, even kings and saints performed Ganesh pooja to complete the Yagna successfully. That's why it is said that before worshiping any God, you should first worship Ganesha so that worshiping that particular God is successful. Worshiping a specific god can bring you great rewards, but the key is to do it successfully. Some people undergo intense austerities for days and months to ensure their worship is obstacle-free; they begin with Ganesh pooja.

c.   Shiva Shakthi

Your ultimate goal is mukti, and to reach this goal, you must complete prarabdha. To exhaust prarabdha, your dominant need, you have to be a certain way. However, some of your past karma strings may act as obstacles, like unnecessary baggage that keeps you from moving in that direction. It's essential to remove those strings that are obstacles and unnecessary. One powerful way to release unnecessary karma is by engaging in rituals at the Lord Shiva temple, such as pouring water on the Lingam. The water holds your memory, and by pouring it on the Lingam, you can remove some unnecessary karma. This allows you to leave your unnecessary baggage behind, making it easier for you to move in the direction you want to. Even if you cannot pour water on the Lingam in every Shiva temple, you can still perform some ritual to leave something of yourself behind. Shiva, known as nirguna, is there to guide you and help you set yourself free from your karma and baggage.

On the other hand, you do not have the necessary energy to fulfill your dominant need. To gain that energy, you worship Shakti. This is similar to the relationship between the Japanese yen and Yan Shiva and Shakti. Shiva removes unnecessary things, whereas Shakti gives you the necessary power.

Each temple is meticulously designed to harness a specific energy that influences people's lives. With countless temples and diverse practices, individuals with varying needs seek fulfillment through different means. By selecting a deity or type of austerity based on your needs, you can gradually attain tranquility and ultimately achieve Brahman.

CHAPTER 6.7. DEALING WITH ELEMENTS: AIR, WATER, SOIL, FIRE, AND SKY.

Treating life-making material poorly and expecting beautiful things from it is stupidity—taking charge of elements is the most fundamental form of yoga. - by Sadguru.

Not for any god. It's the basis of survival, so you bow down to it. Neglecting to manage our resources can lead to diseases and health issues, specifically chronic diseases, which usually last three months or longer and may worsen. You can manage these conditions but cannot cure them entirely; however, by managing the materials properly, you can avoid such diseases and, with some processes, come out of them.

You are the embodiment of your parents, and your guru's memories and influence are integral to who you are. Consider the example of Lord Hanuman, who had a child from his sweat, showing that memory can take forms other than semen. Similarly, Veera Bhadra and Shivangi are said to have originated from a small branch of Lord Shiva's hair, known as Jata. The transmission of memory happens through elements.

The incarnation of Lord Vishnu brought liberation (mukthi) to many demons. These demons were trapped in a relentless cycle, much like Mahishasura, and could not break free. Overcoming their impulses allowed them to attain divinity, but their repetitive nature caused suffering to others. Unfortunately, no one could help them while they were stuck in this cycle.

a.   Water. There is taste because there is water.

Have you ever noticed in movies and TV shows how saintly characters always carry metal vessels filled with water? They use the power of water as a medium for their intentions. Whether it's to curse or bless someone, they use water as a tool to convey their divine energy. They take some water in their palm, utter a mantra, and pour it on them; it's how they curse. They even sprinkle water on their food before eating, so it will positively affect their bodies. Water responds differently based on what it is exposed to, like vibration. Vibrations can come from even the smallest things, such as touch, sound, emotion, a look, or just presence. Similarly, sacred memory comes into theerth from the deity. Different theerth does different things to oneself, and that's the reason there are different temples and processes.

Up to 70 percent of your body is water; it plays a significant role in life, and if it doesn't respond well to you, then your life is done. Handling water properly takes care of the physical body, allowing you to manage other aspects more easily, such as psychological and emotional well-being. That's why you should avoid drinking directly from the tap. Instead, collect the water in a copper, brass vessel, or clay pot, keep it undisturbed, let it settle for some time, and then drink it. This process allows the water to rid itself of any negativity. In the past, people performed rituals that included this water treatment method. Our attitude toward water influences its energy. Just as our thoughts can affect our brains, they can also impact water. Drinking water with gratitude can have a significant effect. Ideally, you should drink water using your hands. If that's impossible, hold the glass or container with both hands while drinking. How a person is giving the food or water, also make a difference.

b.   Air.

When dealing with mental illness, it's essential to consider both medication and therapy. For a mental illness, a psychiatrist prescribes medicines, whereas a psychologist treats with therapy. The psychologist helps the client look at things in a different way or in a way that the person themselves cannot see, being caught in the problem, and assists them in improving their life and relationships. Psychologists who provide therapy often recommend meditation as one of the ways to address mental illness. Mental illness is often described as a disorder indicating a lack of order in the mind and thought processes. Meditation offers a solution by bringing order to this chaos, relieving the mind's constant chatter, and allowing for the proper organization of thoughts. Most meditation techniques, such as pranayama, are breath-based, recognizing the close relationship between the mind and breath.

The quality of the air you breathe is not the only essential factor; the way you breathe is equally important. It is said that those who have mastered the five vayus can avoid psychological problems. Remember, taking care of Prana's breath can help you steer clear of psychological issues, underscoring the importance of your breathing habits for your well-being.

When your mind is out of control, it tends to wander into the past and future, causing you to worry about all kinds of possible and impossible outcomes. However, focusing on your breath can significantly reduce mental activity, allowing you to let go of unnecessary concerns and concentrate on what truly matters. Many have found that this practice has significantly improved their productivity at work. It's not just about spending a few minutes each day on this practice; it's about dedicating intense focus for a few minutes so that you can carry this breathing practice with you throughout the day.

Pranayama is a method to control the five vayus, which are different types of air in the body. Each vayu is related to a specific function in the body. Prana is related to respiratory activity and thought processes. If prana is absent, it means the person is dead. Samana is responsible for generating heat in the body; once it recedes, the body starts getting cold. Apana, when absent, leads to a loss of sensory activity. Medically, it is diagnosed as death, but there are two things in the body that are done with Apana. Udhana, when absent, leads to a heavy feeling in the body. Vyana is a preservative; once it is lacking, the body starts to decay, which may take up to 14 days. Pranayama will improve physical and psychological well-being.

c.   Earth.

Earthing or grounding has recently become popular. It means getting in touch with the soil. It's essential to keep in touch with nature; our soles and palms are designed to interact with the soil through specialized vessels known as AVAs, which efficiently remove excess heat. They must come in contact with the soil because this is the basis of life. There are many health problems that doctors may have difficulty diagnosing. Initially, your doctor may think it's one problem, but after a course of medication, it may be a different problem altogether, because our system is getting confused due to the loss of connection with the soil.

Inflammation is a process through which the body's defense mechanism fights external ailments and heals injuries. There are two types of inflammation: beneficial inflammation, which helps the body heal, and harmful inflammation, which can lead to autoimmune conditions and other diseases. The causes of harmful inflammation are not fully understood, but it is believed that the immune system becomes confused and starts attacking the body. One hundred years ago, almost 90% of people used to sleep on the floor, and very few people had the opportunity to sleep on a wooden bed. This bed concept is foreign to us because the soil absorbs heat from the body, making it necessary in some cold-climate countries where people could not sleep on the floor.

Spending just a few minutes to an hour in contact with soil can work wonders for your well-being. This simple practice has been shown to reduce inflammation, increase blood flow, and boost energy levels. Some researchers even suggest that we may not need as much food as we think but instead need to "charge up" by increasing our cellular energy. After all, reduced cellular energy is often the root cause of weakness and various health issues. Going barefoot is a natural way to stay connected with the earth, as wearing shoes is considered unnatural and can lead to chronic pain and balance issues. This simple change could make a difference, potentially alleviating knee and lower back pain.

d. Fire.

The sun, or fire, is the element that regulates your metabolism. Jatharagni, the fire in your belly, is crucial in digesting food and transforming it into essential components such as blood, flesh, bones, and semen. By illuminating the lamp and basking in sunlight, you can effectively regulate the production of digestive enzymes, crucial for breaking down food and enhancing nutrient absorption. A well-functioning Jataraagni fuels your inner drive to take action in the external world. It symbolizes willpower, signifying a strong desire to achieve an immense potential to conquer the world. Conversely, an inactive Jataraagni leads to a lack of direction and purpose, making individuals susceptible to external influences. Due to low self-esteem, they struggle to embrace or reject opportunities and shy away from assuming responsibilities. Furthermore, poor Jataraagni activity can lead to health issues related to the stomach.

Chitaagni Intellect: When intellect is on fire, it becomes singularly focused, disregarding basic needs such as hunger and procreation. Lost in its pursuit of perfection, it becomes oblivious to the passage of time or any other bodily requirements. It requires external intervention to bring it back to the present.

Bhootaagni elemental fire. When it is on, they have control over their lives and deaths.

e. Askash Sky

Akasha sky Brahmana is in the form of the soul, along with all the other sources that the aatman experiences.

Akasha Ether or space. There is not much you can do about this element. If you take care of the other elements, this will be taken care of automatically, especially when taking care of the fire element in the system. 12 to 18 inches for everybody; that's what we call personal space.

Simple is a shower, not just for cleaning the body, but it rejuvenates and cleanses you. Something that is attached to you is released and gone. Standing up on self is strong, very relatively warm, or cold death life.

Elements which hold the memory.

Salt: Have you ever heard the saying that the character of the person whose salt you consume reflects on your character? The character is influenced not only by being in someone's presence but also by transmitting karmic memories from one person to another. That is why there used to be small traditions like never exchanging salt hand to hand. You have to keep it on the floor; another person will take it. The same applies to elements like sesame seeds and sesame seed oil. These same elements are used to leave out bad karmic memories within, like pouring sesame seeds and oil on a particular deity, pouring water on shivling, and so on. To achieve a particular goal or desired state, having certain things and avoiding others is necessary. To leave out what is not required and open a possibility, there used to be traditions like donating certain food grains austerities.

CHAPTER 6.8. HOME

There is a whole science to properly making homes based on alignment, structure, and colors, and this subject is called Vastu.

Vastu means making your home correctly according to directions. The physical universe is all about geometry. How long and well something functions depends on geometry. Yoga focuses on aligning our physical space with the higher cosmic space. In the same way, Vastu or Agamashastra involves constructing a house that connects with the universe. The physical environment you live in can either support or hinder your journey to becoming your ideal self. A Vastu expert can assist you in optimizing your living space.

The shapes and forms in your environment can affect you. Studies show a consistent correlation between cluttered spaces and depression, such as a lack of motivation and disorganization of the mind. It's essential to keep your home tidy, especially your clothes and bedding, as they can help clear your mind. Additionally, the design of objects around you matters; in ancient times, all the vessels and glass were more spherical than cylindrical.

The center of the house is called Nabi, and from there, energy spreads out in all directions. The type of energy varies in different areas of the home. Sitting in various spots can influence different ways of thinking, both positive and negative. So, if you're feeling down, look at where you're sitting and try to find a more comfortable and pleasant spot.

Most issues are solvable without needing to change the house itself.

Color Shape alignment

Color greatly impacts psychology, affecting our feelings and moods. It can influence how we breathe, demonstrating its effect on emotions. Vastu Shastra suggests painting the whole house in neutral white, with one wall painted in a color linked to the weak planet in the owner's birth chart. This helps balance the home's energy, making it beneficial for the person living there. If unsure which color to choose, it is safest to paint the entire house in neutral colors like white. Based on the light the object reflects, we say that is the color of that particular object. White reflects all light, while black absorbs all light. If you want to absorb everything, use black. If you wish to reflect everything and do not wish to accumulate anything, use white.

Different directions are associated with different elements and colors.

The south is linked to the fire element and is represented by the color red, which symbolizes rajas guna. This color encourages people to dance, drink, and fight, making it beneficial for those who want to gain fame. The east is associated with the air element and is represented by the color green. This direction is favorable for couples and those in marketing, as it relates to networks and connections. The northern element is water, represented by the color blue, which encourages communication. The space is white, symbolizing the west. White creates a sense of openness in the west, and if other colors are present, they won't have much effect. The southwestern direction is associated with yellow earth, which can be yellow or beige.

Roof height.

We see mental space similarly to how we see physical space. A tall ceiling benefits creative individuals and tasks, while a lower ceiling is better for logical and analytical work. A high ceiling is suggested for overall well-being.

Certain plants inside the house have significance. Traditionally, in the southern part of India, we have a plant called Tulasi in front of most houses.

CHAPTER 6.9. IMP RITUALS, ALSO KNOWN AS SAMSKARAS.

a.   Jatakarma Sanskar / Birth ritual

Celebrating birth—After the baby is born, a special ceremony welcomes the new arrival. The father softly speaks a prayer into the baby's ear, creating a moment for the father and child to connect. The father also touches the baby's lips with honey and ghee to welcome them.

b.   Namakrma Sanskar, Naming a child.

The Sanskrit language is not created from imagination; it is created by observing the universe. - Sadghuru.

The sounds impact the creation of forms depending on the frequencies, and at the same time, forms possess a sound. The sound is mantra, and the corresponding form is yantra. Based on this science, people decide what sound is best for a person. A person is born in a certain way and desires to accomplish certain things in his life, so you give him a sound that matches this person's inner self and opens a possibility. When everyone calls that person with that sound, it impacts them positively and enhances them. Usually, two names are given to a person: 1. what works best for the person, and 2. a pet name that creates a harmonious environment in the home. Even the same god is said to react and impact differently when you call him by different names. There used to be a lot of research on naming a child, so the reverberation matches who he is and enhances him. While initiating into the path of liberation, people are given different names. Naming incorrectly can have an adverse effect, often leading to conflicting personalities.

c.   Vidyarambha or Vedaaramba: Upanayana

Vidhyaramba is a ceremony held at age 5 to honor the beginning of learning. While initiating a child for education, they say Aham brahmasmi, incubating the idea that the child's identity is with the entire universe. Because the person will learn valuable skills, we use our skills to protect our identity. Upanayana, or the sacred thread ceremony, signifies a connection to the guru or divine. Vedaramba marks the start of Vedic studies. Keshanta refers to the hair-cutting ritual, where a student leaves a small portion of hair on the head. Samavartana signifies the students' return home from the gurukul, indicating they are prepared for the outside world and other rituals.

d.   Vivah Sankar, Wedding.

The couple promises that they will accompany each other in all pursuits of life: Dharma, Artha, Kama, and Moksha. The marriage process is conducted in a specific manner to ensure that both individuals are connected at their energy level. The energies of the two individuals merge, creating an inseparable bond. This union is designed to foster a sense of exclusivity, allowing them to focus on other aspects of life with stability and commitment.

e.   Anthyesti Sanskar, / Death Rituals.

What remains after death are tendencies, not a conscious mind. The ritual after death is to put some positivity into the tendencies. Some positivity into the vortex after the death of the fish because it takes a new body depending on the tendencies. Tendencies mean no conscious mind to choose. The body can still take action despite being caught in the vortex, as long as it's alive. Despite being in the vortex, the body can counteract the forces and eventually decelerate the vortex, but once the body perishes, it simply becomes circulating water, mere inclinations. Often, the tendencies of a person continue to rotate around their loved ones after death. After conducting death rituals, the tendencies continue to move on their path. It's a way of conveying to the deceased that our relationship persists until your body is alive; once death happens, you go on your way, and it's good for both of us.

A famous Hollywood star lost his son, and even after several years, he continued to see his son and felt his presence. Following a recommendation, he carried out pinda pradhan (death ritual in Hinduism) at Kashi,

India, and found relief. Pinda pradhan and tharpana leave water by hand. If you do not perform the rituals, the memory of the dead will impact you. You may have difficulty moving forward in your life in the direction you wish to go.

CHAPTER 6.10. GURU

Adhyapak is the individual who imparts information, while Upadhyay is the one who integrates information and knowledge. A pandit possesses profound knowledge in a specific subject, and an Aacharya teaches specialized skills. Dhrishta is recognized for having a visionary perspective. A Guru is someone who can genuinely guide you toward liberation, having experienced Brahman. Adhyapak, Upadhyaya, Pandit, and Acharya may serve as teachers but cannot be gurus, whereas gurus can embody all these roles.

The majority of individuals are not in pursuit of a guru but are rather seeking resolutions to their problems. These resolutions may manifest in the form of informative guidance, educational mentors, and individuals who provide them with a sense of direction. Therefore, instructors cater to specific requirements. It is a fact that everything one seeks is in pursuit of fulfillment. This quest for fulfillment ends only with liberation, so everyone is seeking a guru in some form or another.

Some people are not searching for liberation, but they have a need for knowledge about life, death, and what lies beyond. Understanding these concepts is crucial for them to move forward in their journey. Reading scriptures and consuming spiritual content is their preferred method, as the modern world values reasoning and self-education. Embrace scripture reading as a way to gain insight and wisdom. If you are seeking survival, then you should not seek a guru; you should seek a teacher who can help you survive and give you solace. Most people who provide you with psychological solace you consider a guru, but a guru's only interest is in liberating people.

The spiritual process is always tied to individual temperament, and the same applies to the guru. If the guru does not resonate with you, it is advisable to patiently wait for the right spiritual guide. While following a guru can lead you toward spiritual growth, it is important to acknowledge that there may be other aspects of your being that yearn to explore different paths. There exists within you a desire to pursue your unique spiritual journey. You cannot attain Brahman by copying the guru; you must perform your own actions. The guru has attained a higher state that you have not reached, which is why the guru imparts different teachings to different disciples. Whether a guru is really necessary depends on the path you choose. If you wish to learn kriya yoga, also called tantra sadhana, a guru is a must, as an improper way of sadhana can lead to malefic effects. We have fancy ideas about the guru, but the guru can be very simple, and it is also said that the guru is already made for you.

Each consequence described above falls into its own field of subjects. This is basic, perhaps the most important, information.

CHAPTER 7

IMPORTANT POINTS

We have seen what Brahman is and how the systems, processes, and culture lead beings to their ultimate state. Keeping that in mind, we will reverse-engineer some verses from the Geeta and some important points made by many gurus previously.

If Vedanta digests within you, it gives you strength; you will be fearless.

Many people believe that reading the Bhagavad Gita (Geetha) will lead individuals to become saints or that they should strive to become saints by leaving everything behind and living an ascetic life on a mountain. However, the most critical aspect of the Gita is to realize Brahman and perform karma—fulfilling one's societal duties and responsibilities. Remember the first chapter, which talks about decision-making and suffering? Where there is confusion, there is fear, but where there is clarity, there is no fear, even in the face of death. Vedanta provides clarity about life, and for some, Vedanta alone is enough to realize Brahman and be free from all bondages. Regardless of the outcome, or at least for some individuals, this clarity helps them understand where they are in life and take the necessary steps to reach their fulfillment.

Sravana Manana Nidhidhyasa–Nature Vignanamaya.

Once, while Aadi Shankaracharya was traveling, a man in well-dressed clothes came to him and bowed down to Shankaracharya. Then Shankaracharya asked what he had learned. The man replied that he had learned Chathurvedam, Ashta Upanishad, etc. The man humbly added that despite his learning, he was just a shoe mender in front of Shankaracharya. Then Shankaracharya replied, "Yes, you have learned very well about yourself; you are a shoe mender." The man then glared at him. Shankara continued, "Have you people observed him and how he is changing colors?" I said only what he said, but he couldn't digest it. He highlighted that only what is truly understood and assimilated is real Advaita and of actual use.

The learning process involves Sravana, Manana, and Nidhidhyasa. Sravana means listening, observing, and understanding. Then, there's Manana, the practice of reinforcing the understood concepts. This practice leads to further knowledge by asking questions and, eventually, Nidhidhyasa. Converting the information into skill is Manana. Remember, it's essential not just to accumulate knowledge but also to learn and apply it. Learning and not doing anything leads to fear, shame, and guilt. Nidhidhyasa: Gathered information is sunk deep into the mind; then one becomes fearless.

2. The biggest sin is not performing karma. You are neither going up nor down—going up is what we seek. Sometimes, going down can also teach you how to be and how not to be. Even when Arjuna chooses to abstain from war, he is doing karma. Abstaining from doing something is also karma. Understanding 'karthavya' is crucial. It's about doing your own without obstructing others. However, there are instances where conflicts arise, such as when your 'karthavya' and another person's 'karthavya' clash. This is known as 'dharma Sondheim,' which leads to debate and requires careful consideration before proceeding with our duties.

3. Follow the dharma from the core of your heart.

In India, truth always lies within each individual. If something doesn't resonate with your true self, it's not true. There are two aspects to this concept. First, there is consciousness or Brahman, which has been a part of you through many lifetimes, even when you inhabited different forms. It exists both within and outside of you, and in a way, it's everywhere. Secondly, it's only valid if something is proper to your inner self. Everyone is in a different state, seeking different things to fulfill their lives.

Being truthful is the most essential thing. Only then can we move in further directions. Only when you are honest and thoroughly enjoy yourself will you sink into vignanamaya? E.g., Sravana Manana Nidhidhyasa. Unless you digest the desire for that thing into your deep self, it will not end. It may continue many times, and unknowingly, we might roam in the same circle, following the same pattern repeatedly in many lifetimes.

4. Why should we perform karma without expecting anything?

You have the right to perform duties, but not on the results of actions. Do not let the fruits be the purpose of your actions so you won't be attached to not doing your duty. When you are connected to something again, it will lead to repetitiveness. You don't have control over the outcome; you have control over yourself. You have control over the process you go through for the outcome.

Sthithapragna (Thuriya) refers to a person who is equanimous and devoid of emotion in all emotional states. Giving energy to emotions and feelings can lead to repetitive cycles. Shiva is nirguna because he is free from repetitiveness. The individual who attains gnana and internalizes it becomes the fourth person, known as Thuriya. This person witnesses three different states of consciousness: dream, sleep, and wakefulness. Thuriya witnesses all three forms.

5. Showing great skill in wrong and immoral activities is bad, but skillfulness is good.

In a way, karma yoga is a form of yoga of skill. Many nations possess nuclear weapons, either producing them domestically or acquiring them from other sources. They invest huge amounts of money and effort in them. However, there is a very rare probability that they will use those weapons. Then why do they prepare them? Just as a security measure. You know, dharma; you would do what is necessary, regardless of the outcome—but competence also plays a crucial role. You are not competent, but if you go in fearless, then you may end your life.

6. The ultimate gave you buddhi with which you made yourself, at the end of your life, your taste smell (Ruchi Vasana) that decided your life in the next life. Death is just a trace; the flowers turn into fruit, and the flower dies.

The repetitiveness of one's inner core determines one's nature. Man has many forms of memory, which means many layers of repetitiveness. Once death occurs, it's the end for the outer layer; the body stops reproducing itself. However, the underlying repetitiveness persists and determines the form of the next life. According to Buddhist beliefs, if a man is cruel and wild, he will most likely take a life as an animal in his next life. The outer layer is the human body, whereas the deeper layer is cruel, similar to animals. Once the outer layer ends, the inner layer will find expression by choosing its most suitable outer layer.

Your future life is defined by your core nature, and your nature will be defined by the karma you accumulate.

Karma is your making, whether conscious or unconscious. You are performing some karmic action, and that registers deep inside your memory.

7. First, pain and grief will destroy us. Those who caused us pain may suffer something else, so stop crying (shloko nashahithe dhyram). There is no enemy greater than grief. In grief, we will lose our courage, knowledge, and skills.

8. People look down upon the mind, money, and resources in spiritual processes.

Consciousness reflects through the body, mind, and energy. By retrieving your attention from the body and mind, you become more conscious. If you wish to move forward on a spiritual path and use meditation techniques, distancing yourself from worldly things like the body and mind is beneficial. However, if you are living in society, don't ever say that money, property, and the entire concepts learned over years of practice are of no use. The mind is seen as an enemy by some on the spiritual path, and they want to kill it. When a time bomb is ticking, you cannot meditate because it is the mind that reminds you of the situation. Trying to stop the mind is not a solution; instead, focus the mind on solving the problem.

There are enlightened masters who, by retrieving attention from the body and mind, attain Samadhi. However, when they have to teach those lessons to others, they must use the same body, mind, and language. There are some exceptions, like telepathy. That's probably the reason I see many gurus as experientially energy-wise wonderful, but one of their disciples makes their guru famous because they are too intelligent and communicative and take the message of the guru into the world.

CHAPTER 8

CONCLUSION

Spiritual conclusion

There are a number of ways to reach the ultimate; according to the Shiva Purana, Shiva taught 112 ways to reach the ultimate. Later, based on the time, place, and planetary positions, they were divided into several more. After calculating various forces, a method was used in a particular geographical location for a specific time. Because in that place and time, the nature of the people was a certain way, they were drawn to certain things. That is why different Dharmas started for different periods. Also, dharma processes are sometimes created because of the prime influence of political conditions. Whether from this country or a Far East country, Lord Rama, Krishna, or anyone who reached the ultimate is like a god and could be a Guru. You follow your guru's path and make your way forward. Different gurus taught different methods based on various factors like political reasons, planetary positions, and geographical location.

Suppose a guru brought a method into practice, and the guru passed away sometime later. After 100 years, the method became popular and gained 10,000 followers. There is another method with 12,000 followers and another with 10,000 followers. After some time, someone gave these methods the names Religion A, Religion B, and Religion C. Thus, the fight between religions seems like my method versus yours. Sanathana says that all religions are methods to reach the ultimate.

The system is designed to help individuals reach their Liberation. Everyone can progress in their own way. If it is not possible, they should be doing something that will move them one step closer. Anything considered beneficial for an individual is also said to contribute to their continued existence and guide them towards Liberation. Understanding karma involves acknowledging the role of free will. This understanding helps to eliminate confusion and enables individuals to take responsibility for their actions. With this insight, one can confidently and purposefully work towards their karma.

Non spiritual conclusion

We can categorize people into three distinct types. The first type embodies the qualities of Dhuryodhana, who takes great pride in himself and is willing to fight for every little thing that concerns his pride without considering all aspects and without much concern for others. The second type is like Arjuna, who is strong, knowledgeable, and has the support to kill everyone on the battlefield.

He can do what he has to, but he is always confused and has inner conflicts and moral dilemmas. He thinks along these lines: "Is this good? They are all my brothers, fathers, and gurus. What will I do with all the kingdom and luxury?" It is not that he cannot win; it is just that after winning, he feels guilty about his victory. Deep down, those who wish for failure cannot win—the victory where there is the suffering of other people. The third type, reflecting Krishna's characteristics, demonstrates a deep understanding of what needs to be done in any given situation and exhibits a clear and unwavering resolve to take necessary action. The problem is that most Indians fall into the Arjuna category, a confused mind.

In a society that profits from your self-doubt, liking yourself is a rebellious act.

(2022). Structural Analysis and Design of Fasteners on Steel for Software Implementation. https://core.ac.uk/download/532933960.pdf

Society likes only the people at a crossroads, contemplating which direction to take. In this way, it can interact with you and effectively persuade you to make a choice. It doesn't appreciate those who take a firm stand; often, society uses distorted spirituality as a way to control individuals.

I do not write this book to impose spirituality on anyone. I aim to provide clarity and share insights that make sense to my logical reasoning. It is an attempt to help people free themselves from their inner struggles. If my explanation of concepts like karma, Brahman, and the processes does not resonate with you, then you are free in one way because there are only four consequences for you. You manage those four to the fullest. The art of war, or Chanakya neethi to some extent, could be the best thing for you because it offers valuable wisdom for navigating life's challenges for atheists. You don't have to feel conflicted between the sacred and the sinner. If my reasoning resonates with you and sheds light on how things work, you are free to take action on your terms. Either way, it should set you free.

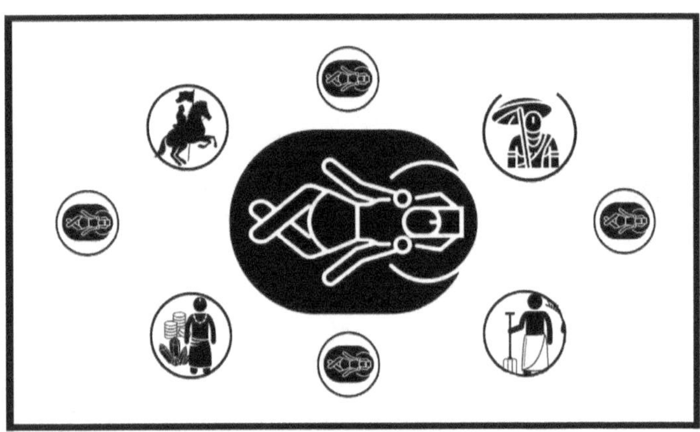

* 9 7 8 9 3 4 8 1 9 9 6 1 4 *